Are You Living YOUR Best Dash?

Mariesa Moore-Gentry

Published by
StarksNest Publishing
a division of Olive Tree Resources, Inc
www.olivetreepartner.com

Your Best Dash
www.yourbestdash.com

ISBN: 978-1-966229-01-8 (paperback)
Printed in the United States

Cover design and photography by
John Brown
"Brown Boy Graphics & Photography"

Makeup done by
Natashia White-Pass
"Blushed by Natashia"
Co-Owner of Face Cafe Glam Bar
Raleigh, NC

For my Dad and Mom
Ronald Laverne Henry and LaVeta Eileen Henry
My world and my heart
Thank you for always loving, encouraging,
supporting,
and forgiving me.
I am, because of you.

Love Your Daughter,
Mariesa LaRonda Henry – Mariesa LaRonda Moore-Gentry
4/11/1984　　　　　Currently Living My Best Dash

ACKNOWLEDGEMENTS

To God: My dear Heavenly Father, You are my entire world. Thank you for Your continual forgiveness. You love me with all my flaws and still call me worthy. Thank you for being my provider, my peace, my comfort, my joy, my reason for it all! You have kept me even when I didn't want to be kept. You have inclined Your ear to me when I couldn't even utter the words to say because the pain was so great. You are patient and understanding. You are not like man and I thank you. I am confident in whom You created me to be, and I thank you for the calling on my life. My desire is to make you smile and walk in the purpose you have for me. I praise You, and I worship You with my life. I love you! In Jesus' name, Amen.

To my husband: Thank you for being you. You listen during my venting sessions and encourage me along the way. You work hard to make sure that the children and I are well taken care of. As a result of you working so hard, I had the time to go after my God-given dreams and passions. Thank you for allowing me to share a small snippet of my (our) story. You didn't give up on us during those rough patches. You stuck and stayed even if giving up seemed like the easy way out. Your love for me is so evident and I'm grateful to be able to do life with you. I love you husband!

To my children: Thank you all for bearing with me through this process. You challenge me to be better every day. You make me laugh even when I am trying to be serious. The four of you are truly my inspiration. I keep going and reaching for my goals because I know that you all are watching. There is nothing that you can't do and never let anyone, and I mean anyone, tell you anything different. Each one of you is special and unique. Individually, you have a purpose that only you can fulfill. You are beautiful inside and outside. You are who God says you are and nothing different. Go after your dreams even if you have to go alone, but as long as I'm here, you won't have to go after them alone. I will always be your #1 supporter, your best friend (after God), and your biggest cheerleader. You each make me so proud to be your mother. I thank God for the blessing of my children. Each of you holds a piece of my heart and from my love you will never part. I love you ALWAYS!

To my siblings: Thank you for the endless support you have given me since day one. There is no one else in the entire world quite like the two of you. We understand each other on a level that no one else will ever understand. The values and principles that were instilled in us to stick together is a rare find. You both provide peace and refuge for me. We have shared in some of the same unexplainable pains and rejoiced in some of the same victorious triumphs. Thank you for encouraging, helping, and loving me. Seeeeeester, thank you for helping edit the book. I know it wasn't something that was in your agenda (smile), but I appreciate you taking the time to help me. You have no idea how much it means. It goes without saying, but I love you both!

To my family and friends: You know who you are, yes you. Thank you for your encouragement. God has blessed me with some of the most caring, loving, and genuine people. Thank you for helping me, listening to me day in and day out concerning this book, and just being there to cheer me on. I love you all dearly.

To my counselor/therapist: God knew what I needed and when I needed it. You are an answer to my prayers. Thank you for walking in your purpose and for being passionate about what God has for you to do. Thank you for speaking life into my life and helping me put the pieces back together again. I will forever be grateful for you.

To Dr. Shad: Thank you for inspiring me before you even knew I existed. I'm grateful for how you follow God and allow Him to lead you to help others. The impact that your works have made in my life are priceless. After I spoke with you during my certification interview, I cried like a baby. I will always remember those tears of joy I shed due to your words of encouragement you spoke over my life. Thank you, thank you, thank you!

To my publisher: April, thank you so, so, so much! You have no idea how much of a superwoman you are to me! You let me babble on and on in conversations to get all these ideas out my brain, all the while patient, loving and so encouraging. You never allowed me to wonder what my next move was, and you never left me to think you forgot about me. Thank you for being there! You took time out of your busy schedule to make sure I was set, settled, and always moving forward. I am grateful for all the work that you have put in to make sure my vision became a reality. Thank you for following after God's heart and for the impact you have on others as a result. You are amazing and I believe the best is yet to come for you and your family. I love you April. I'm so glad that we are now forever connected.

To YOU: Yes, you! Thank you much for purchasing this book. I pray that you are inspired and encouraged as you read. May God continue to bless you.

TABLE OF CONTENTS

FOREWORD

I am always inspired when someone not only lives out their 'dash' in life with exuberance but recognizes what the dash means to them while they're going through it. It is a wise person who understands what life is really all about. And I am especially inspired when someone puts it into words, and brings the message to life, as Mariesa has done so well in these pages.

The reader will relate personally to much of the story the author tells. Blending her insights with spiritual values, Mariesa shares the practical ideas that helped guide her through it all.

Mariesa is a life coach, certified through the Life Coach Institute. It was through working with that organization that I first became familiar with Mariesa and her remarkable ability to help people turn failings or setbacks into triumphs. You will recognize her life coaching spirit and encouraging solutions throughout the book. She challenges you to make your life work every day, in the highest possible way, and she gives you page after page of practical steps to help you do exactly that.

I know you're going to enjoy the time you spend with Mariesa—the person, the spiritual teacher, and the life coach. You'll find her questions filled with thoughtful guidance, and that her faith-filled optimism is contagious. What she suggests to you, she lives herself and proves time and time again that it works. Enjoy the journey and get ready for some life improvements.

Shad Helmstetter, Ph.D.
August 2019

INTRODUCTION

———

Many years ago, I remember my father eulogizing someone. He delivered many eulogies, but one sticks out in particular. He drew the audience's attention to the front of the program and to the dates on it. There was a date on which the person was born, and the other showed us when they died. The small, sometimes overlooked detail that was most significant, was the dash between the dates. I know that we're familiar with the dash and what it represents, but what I don't understand, is how we can treat it as if it's insignificant.

It usually takes a term of approximately nine months for a dash to begin but only one second for it to end. We must not take it for granted. My questions to you are: "How are you living your dash?" and "Are you living it to the fullest?" The second question is a little cliché. Furthermore, what does that even mean? I thought it was important to ask because I want to give my thoughts on living your dash to the fullest. You only get one, right? In this dash, there will be excitement, devastation, breath-taking moments, and life-changing occurrences.

We are not able to control everything that comes our way, but what we can control is our response. This book was birthed after I had endured some of the most difficult of life's contractions. When in the midst of the excruciating pain and uncertainty, I had no idea of how God was still working in my life. One particular night, I remember I couldn't sleep. As I laid there, He spoke words to my heart that I quickly wrote down. I didn't know that these words would soon be developed over some time into this book.

Something which stuck out in this writing journey that I held onto was: "It's not even about you." I would hear this in my heart when I felt like throwing in the towel and scrapping the book. I reminded myself that God didn't heal me and bring me through to victory just for me. I kept going for you. God gave me the strength I needed for you. I pray that this book ministers to your heart, that it gives you a renewed sense of self, and pushes you to live YOUR BEST DASH! So please, go with me as I take you on this short journey about living.

Chapter One
YOLO Dash – Living with No Regrets

Your past shaped who you are today,

But remember that your past doesn't have the final say.

When I had my second child, I decided to get an epidural as I did with my first child. As they were prepping me to put this long, stare-at-it-like-a-deer-in-headlights-when-you-see-it needle in my spine, I thought twice about the decision to even have it done again. But then, that crippling labor pain hit and my reservations about it went out the door. "Hit me! Hit me quick!" I went ahead, hunched over that pillow and breathed like never before. All the while, I was praying that these beasts called contractions would just stop until after my wonderful pain relief had been completely secure. Ha! Yeah right!

As I hunched over that pillow, those contractions came as if I welcomed them with open arms. As they applied the antiseptic solution to clean the epidural site and "numbed" the area, my heart pounded. I told myself that it would be over in just a few short minutes. *Mariesa, breathe and relax. This too shall pass!* I kept talking to myself and to God when all of a sudden, I felt pain! Not labor pain, but somethin'-ain't-right pain. I heard the doctors behind me in confusion as they quickly pulled the needle out my back. Something didn't go right, and I felt it. I literally felt the sharp pain as that attempt to insert the needle was unsuccessful. "Ma'am, we're going to need you to hunch down even more. Really hunker down on that pillow." *Seriously!? Okay Mariesa, you can do this. I can do this, right after this contraction...OOOOUUUUUCH!*

When that contraction passed, the second attempt was made. I felt the pressure of the needle go into my back, but suddenly, there was a sharp pain in my stomach as if the needle hit it from the inside. Before I knew it, I yelled out in pain. *What just happened?* The anesthesiologist removed the needle with such haste. Confusion filled my mind. I told myself that if this third attempt was also unsuccessful, I would tell them to forget it. The pain of the complications was greater than the pain of labor. Thankfully, this attempt was a success, and I gave birth to a healthy baby girl.

When it came time to create a birthing plan with my third child, guess what I didn't want. That's right. An epidural. I wanted to steer away from having to possibly go through the complications of that process again. (Please don't let this scare you if you are an expectant mother or father with an epidural in your plan. My first epidural process was smooth.) Instead, I reached out to an amazing person I knew who was also a doula. I explored the option of a medicinal-free, completely natural birth. This is the route I chose, and I am glad I did. Don't get me wrong, there was much pain. More than I could've ever imagined.

During my labor and delivery, my doula helped me to remain in control of the entire situation. The only things I couldn't control were the contractions and pain of delivery. What I could control was how I reacted to and perceived them. With every contraction that I felt coming on, I was on top of it. As soon as the tightening warning came, I knew that the pain was about to hit. I made sure I sprang into action by breathing steadily and conquering each contraction like the champ I am. Weeks before I went into labor, my doula told me that she would allow me one time to lose it. She said that I only had one time to just spazz out and that was it. With that in mind, I continued to breathe through contraction after contraction. The relief I felt towards the end of each one served as encouragement. I can still see her in my face and hear her in my ear saying, "Slow your breathing down." "You got this!" "Beautiful job!" "You're amazing!" At the end of some of the contractions, the nurse said, "Good job! That's another one gone that you never have to go through again."

At the end of all that pain, mental anguish, fatigue, and bodily trauma, I gave birth to a healthy baby boy. The joy was overwhelming! I gave birth without any medication, and I remained in control of the situation. But what if I had lost control during the pain? I would've still gotten to the end and the result would have been the same, but at what cost? What if I decided to lose control and spazz out for real? What if I made the choice to curse everybody out? What damage could I have done with my words and actions because of the temporary pain? What if I hurt myself or someone else because I was not in control? The contractions of your dash will be great at times, but do you lose control or take control when they come?

When in labor there will be pain, life-altering pain, but how we handle the pain is key. We, as human beings, give birth to many things in our lives: goals, dreams, self-improvement, and the list goes on. There will be contractions that come in order for us to give birth to these "babies." How we handle and perceive every one of life's contractions is key. These snippets of my birthing stories lead me to the point of this first chapter. If I had any regrets, it would be that at various points in my life, I have given control of my thoughts over to outside sources.

LIVING WITH NO REGRETS

Sure, there will be things that we may regret in life. Whether it is something that we have done, something that we have gone through, or something that someone has done to us, we all have regrets. The thing is, we have the power to consciously change in order to create a future with less regrets. I'm not sure about you, but I don't want to leave this earth remorseful, with a long list of things that I didn't do for whatever reason. I am reminded of the Serenity Prayer coined by American theologian Reinhold Niebuhr:

"God, grant me the Serenity to accept the things I cannot change, Courage to change the things I can, and Wisdom to know the difference."

Every now and again, I say this prayer to get through barriers in my mind. There are things in my past that try to haunt me. Our pasts try to haunt us and have us dwelling back in that place that's no longer with us. Either way, it's in the past and it cannot be changed. So, I apply the first line of this prayer to this area of my life. Grant me the serenity to accept the things I cannot change. This is so powerful! So frequently, we dwell on the what ifs and camp in the past as if we can do something about it. We say things like, "I should've decided to wait," "If I could go back and not have eaten all those honey buns, oatmeal cream pies, and ho hos, I wouldn't be this heavy" or "If I would've just married so-and-so, I would have been so much better off" or "I wish I could go back and..." It's gone now! It's time to live in the now and move on!

Just to break it down a little further, serenity is the state of being calm, peaceful, and untroubled. I want to be at peace about my past. Yes, my decisions sucked at various times, I could have eaten a lot better, if I would've married him there may've been issues that I'm not equipped to handle, and yes, I could have done better in a plethora of areas of my life. But what good is it doing me in my now to look back wishing, thinking, hoping, and fantasizing about what could have been? You're absolutely correct in what you just thought...NONE! What could have been is not what is. Additionally, you are losing more of your "now" drooling over the shoulda, woulda, coulda triplets. I love Brian McKnight, and he said it best. "I coulda done this, I coulda done that, but I know I can't go back, cause now it's just too late. I'm saying shoulda, woulda, coulda...yeah."

LIVE IN YOUR NOW

Instead of wasting time looking back, move in your "now!" I heard Willie Moore, Jr. on the radio say that the present is a gift, and that's why it's called the "present." In one second from now, this moment will be gone. So, make sure you remember the importance of your now and how it will shape your future. As of now, I don't have tomorrow. Occasionally, I hear people say, "There's always tomorrow." I have even said this phrase myself, but boy was I wrong! I'm grateful that after I said it, I was actually blessed with it, but tomorrow is not promised to any of us. "Why, you do not even know what will happen tomorrow. What is your life? You are a mist that appears for a little while and then vanishes." (James 4:14 NIV)

On October 22, 2013, I posted a status on Facebook that read, "What's the age range for women to go through a midlife crisis?" Shortly after, a friend of mine, who has now passed on, posted an encouraging message on my timeline as a result of that post. It read, "If you are depressed, you are living in the past. If you are anxious, you are living in the future. If you are at peace, you are living in the present." (-Lao Tzu) At the time of the post, I must have been going through a pretty stressful time. I was either depressed or anxious. When I read this quote, I realized just how powerful it is and that it speaks volumes. It did something to me. It challenged me to make gradual changes. It compelled me to live in my now. I am convinced that the reason that we are depressed in living in the past is because we cannot change it; we can no longer do anything about it. Dwelling there is not healthy, and it restrains you from progressing in your life. You must come out of the bondage of the past.

Don't get me wrong, the past has shaped who you are, how you think, and the path you're on. The past isn't all bad, but that doesn't change the fact that IT DOESN'T CHANGE. Obsessing over the names they called you, completely wallowing in grief for extended amounts of time, holding onto offenses, amongst an abundance of other negatives can literally wreak havoc on your mental health. I could insert a fancy quote or a statistic here, but I'm choosing not to. If you don't believe me, Google it.

LET GO BY ANY MEANS NECESSARY

For those who are hanging onto offenses (clearly, they've already happened, so they're in the past), I have something for you. For the past few years, I've had the privilege of attending church where Bishop Stenneth E. Powell, Sr. has blessed my life tremendously through his teachings and sermons. One particular quote of his that has stayed with me fits so perfectly here. "You will relive the pain each time you replay the offense in your mind." You are subjecting yourself to unwarranted pain each time you think about what they did to you, or in some cases, what you did to yourself.

There are occasions when I would sit and think about how I could have been a better child or teenager growing up. I wasn't what I would say "bad," but I could be cross in my own way. I remember having a bad attitude with my dad and more so with my mom during various instances. I look back, especially now that I'm raising my own teen, and think to myself, I should've been better. I think about how if only I had listened more and been more obedient, a lot of what I have gone through could have been avoided. I wouldn't have dealt with many of the difficulties, mostly in my mind, if only I had... If I decide to stay there in that regret, it will make me sad and consume me to the point where I start to feel down. When I feel down, it takes over my life in that moment and for as long as I stay there.

It robs me of my "now," my gift--the present. Think of that thing that you regret deep down inside or that thing that's holding you hostage to your past: Think of the way it felt for Mama to turn her back and leave you for that man. Think of how you felt when your husband left you and your children for another woman. Think about how you have never even met either of your birth parents because they gave you away when you were born. Think about that thing that brings you to tears and you say to yourself, "If only I had..." "If only they had..." Whatever it may be, if you dwell on it too long, I bet you could sit there and make yourself go into a depression over it. I know that I can.

The pain is present, and it shouldn't be. We did that! We allowed ourselves to replay something that we cannot change. What in the entire world can I do about my childhood and teenage years now at 34 years old? I can't even apologize to my parents now. It's a tactic! Satan doesn't want us to be progressive and get over things, heal and be whole, be delivered and set free, forgive and be forgiven. He wants us bound, unforgiving, resentful, and depressed. He wants us dwelling on the if onlys, the I should'ves, and the they could'ves. He wants you under his control. It starts in your mind! If he can get your mind, he will have ample opportunity to begin the destruction of the other areas of your life. Don't allow that joker to do it!

If the pain is so bad that you cannot get beyond it and you seem to not be able to get free of your past, there is absolutely nothing wrong with seeing a professional counselor. My father used to say that God gives us faith, and He also gives us common sense. If you think you need some help, if you don't really know if you need help, if you know something is not right with you, from the bottom of my heart, I urge you to get help. Commonly, we are bound to the stigmas that have been shaped about counseling and therapy. It is time to cut those strings and grow! Don't let Satan use your mind as his playground!

GUARD YOUR MIND

Towards the end of my father's battle with cancer, nearly 14 years ago, he would ask me to anoint him with oil and pray for his mind. He was mindful of what Satan was trying to do. After numerous years of preaching, teaching, pastoring, and living for God, Satan still wanted to consume his thoughts and have him thinking that God couldn't heal him just because He hadn't. Dad knew better. He knew that God was able, but Satan wanted him to dwell on why He hadn't physically healed his body. We will never understand everything here on earth but hold on to the hope that after a while, you'll understand it better!

"For now we see only a reflection as in a mirror; then we shall see face to face. Now I know in part; then I shall know fully, even as I am fully known." (I Corinthians 13:12 NIV) Hold on to this scripture when the enemy tries to attack your mind with tragedies in your own life that you don't understand. Right now, we can only see so much; our understanding is limited. There will come a time, when things will be revealed to us. When we are joined with our Father in Heaven, our knowledge will become clear. We will see plainly and openly. But for now, know that God is with you, and He knows the plans He has for you. Don't allow Satan or his assistants to tell you otherwise.

DON'T WAIT! ACT NOW!

When my mother was going through her illness, I sat in her bedroom with her, and we had a conversation about what was going on at that time. She was dying. Cancer had invaded her body, and death was lingering like a dark cloud on the gloomiest of days. Through all of that, she remained her sweet and humble self. She thanked everyone for being so nice to her, for helping her, and for being there for her. She never took a kind gesture of any sort for granted. She was such a genuinely grateful person, and I loved it. She never felt entitled or like she should be in the limelight, even as the First Lady of the church my father pastored. As she relayed to me all the love she had been shown, I remember telling her that she was simply reaping what she had sown. Anyone who knew my mother, knows exactly what I'm talking about.

She was the sweetest, most loving, kind-hearted and gentle person you could ever meet. She was the epitome of LOVE. This love was reciprocated to her, especially during this time in her life. My heart was full sitting there listening to her talk about her gratefulness. However, after a while, my heart began to break. Even while I sit here and type, the tears have welled up in my eyes thinking about it. It hurt. To know that my mother had regrets broke my heart. I sat and listened attentively while I controlled my emotions. She listed just a couple of things that she would have done differently or given the chance again, she was going to do after her healing. She was a very soft-spoken, quiet person, and from our conversation that day, she purposed in her mind to be bolder and a little more outgoing.

To me, she was perfect. There are some people who are bold and outgoing who need to be more reserved and be adopted in the "shut mouth" ministry. She may not have even realized what a strong presence she had. She walked in gifts that many do not have. To those around her, she didn't need to change a thing. One day, I had the privilege of speaking about her to a crowd of people. In that tribute, I said that if someone didn't get along with her, it wasn't because of her. She took time with and showed herself friendly and loving to people who the majority of others wouldn't attempt to give the time of day. She was a woman used by God and she moved by His Power.

You never know what a person is dealing with on the inside. I will talk more about this later but for now, the fact that she had regrets really bothered me. It is actually one of the greatest influences for this book. She encouraged me to do what I wanted to do. If there was something that I wanted to do for the Lord or something He was pulling me to do, to go ahead and DO IT. Do not wait! Do not worry! Just get it done!

I encourage and even challenge you today to do what it is that you want to do. Whatever the Lord has called or wants you to do, do it! Don't delay and possibly miss an opportunity set before you. If you have waited years to get to this point of progression, let the past go. Blessedly, you have right NOW! If you are reading this, you have right NOW! Put this book down and write out your goals. They don't have to be perfect, but write them out, no matter what they are, how they may seem trivial or humongous and out of reach. Who are you to say what God can't do? Nothing is out of reach for Him! So please, go ahead and start writing your vision. Chapter Two will be right here waiting when you get back.

Chapter Two
Living My Dash to the Fullest

———

Welcome back! I hope you have written your goals and visions and are ready to move forward in checking each goal off your list with a sense of accomplishment. If you chose not to write or have previously written them, I encourage you to do so or to even revise your goals. When you do this, it (re)focuses and (re)organizes you. You have just begun the first step in what I call living your dash to the fullest.

The second line of the Serenity Prayer reads, "...courage to change the things I can." The only thing YOU can change is your "now" for your future. Sometimes, this takes a lot of courage. Because Satan is sly and cunning, he will try to trick you into thinking that you're disabled, not qualified, less than enough, and not courageous. DO NOT believe his lies. He is the father of all lies. He comes to kill, steal and destroy! He doesn't want you to change, grow, or push towards positivity. No longer will we reside in our pasts that we cannot change! We accept this and we move forward. If you still aren't sure that you can move beyond your past, let me reassure you that you already have. Why? You might ask. My answer is: Because it is already gone, whether you like it or not.

WHAT DOES THAT MEAN?

So, what does it mean to live your "life" to the fullest? This is a catchy phrase that people have been saying down through the years. Upon hearing this, you may visualize a person with a huge smile on their face, holding a wad of money, driving a fancy car and cruising down the street as their life is flawlessly lived. You may even envision a family. This family includes a mother, father, 2.5 children- a boy, a girl and a _____ (I never knew what the .5 was), and a dog. They live in a big, beautiful house with a white picket fence surrounding the property. They drive expensive cars and are extremely successful in their career fields or in their schooling. Some of us may look at this mask of a perfect life and call it success. However, success is measured differently, and it is unique to each of us.

Aforementioned, this phrase is cliché and can be misunderstood, but I hope to successfully and plainly tell what it means to me. It may convey a totally different meaning to others and that is absolutely fine. Living your dash to the fullest may look different from what others perceive to be "the fullest," and we need to be okay with that. We are all different.

WHAT DOES IT LOOK LIKE?

When you live your life to the fullest, it includes **physical exercise**, if you're able. When I get up in the morning, I like to start my day off by walking or jogging. When I do this, my thoughts are more positive, my body feels better, and I usually get more accomplished throughout the day. When you exercise, endorphins are released. If you're not one to take the time to exercise, you have the power to **change** this. Take a few minutes, a few days per week and get a little physical exercise in.

During my morning exercise, I am in my thoughts. Most days, I listen to music also. I worship; I meditate; I think about how I can improve; I think about what I can accomplish on that specific day; I pray. There are times when I think about mistakes I've made and how those mistakes have taken a toll on my life now. At that point, the thoughts begin to spiral until I realize what is really going on. Here I am, trying to be positive and treat my body to life-changing physical activity, and that joker won't leave me alone. So, I quickly redirect myself back to my positive thoughts and resist the trap set before me. See, there will be many times, really too many times, when Satan will interrupt your life with distractions to unfocus you. So, let's talk about mental exercise.

We usually equate being "healthy" with eating nutritious foods and exercising. These necessities are a part of it, but being healthy requires much more. If I am physically fit but constantly feel defeated in my mind, it will eventually take its toll on my physical health. Physical exercise aids tremendously when it comes to your mental state, but it isn't everything. **Mental exercise** is just as important as physical exercise.

Practice positivity and exercise your mentality. You may wonder how you can do this. Trust me, it is easier said than done. Our first reaction to challenging circumstances, accidents, etc. is usually not positive. When you stub your toe on the corner of the dresser, the first thing that comes to your mind or even out of your mouth isn't "Oh goody!" When we are wronged, our first reaction may be to set that person straight or to get revenge. A quote that comes to mind here reads, "Self-control is strength. Right thought is mastery. Calmness is power." (-James Allen) If we can learn to control ourselves, we would be better off. We need to be less reactive and more proactive.

One time, as my children and I traveled back home from a trip, there were a number of traffic jams and people driving crazily. This four-and-a-half-hour trip turned into six hours, and in my frustration, I started to yell and allow my anger to escape my mouth. "This is stupid!" "These people can't drive!" "Go straight!" "What is the hold up?!" "Just go! Uggghhhhh!" As this occurred, my children were listening. At the time, I didn't care because I was in the moment.

Later on, I began to think that in a few short years, my children will have their license(s). If I am ever in the car with them and they start to carry on like I did, how disappointed I would be. First off, it's not safe to be on edge like that when operating a vehicle. Furthermore, what good comes of it? Did I get home any faster? No. Was I pleased with myself after the moment? No. A couple of my children even remarked on my ranting. Afterwards, I felt bad because I didn't practice positivity or patience. I allowed my exhaustion, frustration and road rage to get the best of me that day (and some other days).

So many times, we are faced with issues and disputes that will try to push us over. Learning to have **self-control** and **self-discipline** is key. Being willing to and knowing when to walk away before conflicts escalate are crucial parts of self-discipline. We want to prove our point and get it across to them. We want to give them a piece of our minds. My father used to say not to give people a piece of your mind because you need to keep all the mind you have. It may already be scarce.

I remember a couple years ago when my oldest son pushed me to my limits. Standing there in the kitchen, I looked at the pantry door and there was a scripture I had posted. It read, "A gentle answer turns away wrath, but a harsh word stirs up anger." (Proverbs 15:1 NIV) I read it aloud over and over again. My son wondered why I did this, but he soon got the picture. I was ready to fuss him out and not exercise gentleness, but this Word helped me to refocus and calm down. You may think to yourself that reciting a scripture, phrase or deep breathing doesn't work. Well of course it won't if it's not regularly practiced.

You have to start somewhere. Sometimes, we will fail, and we will "pop off" or allow our emotions to get the best of us. The thing is, another situation is coming. Don't beat yourself up. Move on and get better. You will have opportunity after opportunity to improve your self-control as long as you are living. The more you practice, the better you will become. Frequently, we give up on doing better because it takes work. If you truly want to live your dash to the fullest, **self-improvement** is necessary. Hence, living your life the fullest takes work. The most important thing to remember here is to pray and practice. God will help you. Faith without works is dead.

Establish a routine. Daily, my children and I recite our GOOD MORNING mantra, if you will. Usually, this is done on the way to school. I find that it helps start our day on a positive note and it really helps put things into perspective. This is what is posted on our wall (minus the scriptures):

G-Get up grateful!

O-Open your heart to God.

O-Open your mind to God.

D-Dedicate your day to God.

M-Meditate on God's Word.

O-Optimize your faith and hope.

R-Rebuke all evils.

N-Never doubt God's love.

I-Inspire someone.

N-Nothing should scare you.

G-Go out with joy!

As we recite this, I will say the letters and the children will reply with what they stand for. I also ask questions. It may go something like this:

Me: G!

Children: Get up grateful!

Me: Why?

Children: God gave us another day! We woke up! This is the day the Lord has made! We will rejoice and be glad in it!

Me: Yes, we have never seen this day, (insert day and date) before. Today is unique and not like any other. We are extraordinary and today is an extraordinary day! Today is great because we make it great! O!

Children: Open your heart to God!

Me: God, we open our hearts to You for whatever you have for us today. O!

Children: Open your mind to God!

Me: God, we open our minds to You on today. Please direct our minds and help us to have a positive mindset. D!

Children: Dedicate your day to God!

Me: Why?

Children: God gave us this day, so we give it back to him!

Me: M!

Children: Meditate on God's Word! (We may recite the scripture we are looking at this day.)

Me: O!

Children: Optimize your faith and hope!

Me: That's right! We have humongous hope because we have a great big God! R!

Children: Rebuke all evils!

Me: Yes! We rebuke any evil thoughts that try to enter our minds! We rebuke any evils-things that may come to our minds to do or say, in Jesus' name! N!

Children: Never doubt God's love!

Me: How much does God love us?

Children: So much that He gave His one and only Son that whoever believes in Him won't perish but have eternal life!

Me: Never forget it! I!

Children: Inspire someone!

Me: Encourage somebody. Be a friend. Compliment your teacher. Be helpful. Show God's love. N!

Children: Nothing should scare you!

Me: Why?

Children: Because God has not given us the spirit of fear, but of power, love and a sound mind.

Me: What does sound mind mean?

Children: Self-control!

Me: Good! So, you can control yourself. You cannot control others, but you can control you. G!

Children: Go out with joy!

Me: Yes! Happiness is found in happenings, but joy is found in....

Children: Jesus!

This may seem strange to some, and that's okay. This morning routine in the car really helps us. Try it. It's not just a routine, we are speaking over and setting the tone for our day. I find that it helps me have an attitude of gratitude. When I think about Him waking me up, my heart begins to overflow with gratefulness. I reflect on what could have happened. My heart bows in submission. This time with them helps me in so many ways. While writing this book, the parts that say, "Optimize your faith and hope," "Inspire someone," and "Nothing should scare you," kept me grounded and pushed me to keep writing. If I allowed myself to wallow in musings of failure and unsuccess, I would not have been able to finish this book.

I continued to keep pushing because God had not given me the spirit of fear. I told myself I would not be afraid of not finishing nor would I be afraid of it not inspiring and helping the masses. This self-push, if you will, is a process. There were some days when I didn't write; I didn't even feel like getting out of the bed, but I did anyway. Satan wanted me to be in my feelings. When those moments were gone, I didn't let it affect me in my now. Instead, I pushed. Don't allow your yesterday to determine your today. If yesterday wasn't a progressive or "good" day, it is gone now. Break out of it and keep pushing! If the aforementioned morning routine doesn't work for you, that's fine. Find your own morning inspiration and start your day off with positivity. It really does set your tone for the day.

The next points are to **go after your dreams** and **always be grateful** which we expound upon in Chapters 4 and 6.

Elevate yourself above any problem that may come your way. While driving the other day, God spoke to me about airplanes and elevation. After an airplane takes off, it begins to ascend. In order for it to reach its destination, great altitude must be reached before it can level off. The plane ascends and gets farther and farther from Earth. When I'm on a flight, I prefer to sit next to the window. I like to look out and see the things on Earth "get" smaller and smaller. During my travels, I may even grow excited because of where I'm going. We are just like that airplane in a sense.

As we elevate ourselves above our problems, they seem smaller and smaller. You see, if you can just elevate your mind and focus on God, the smaller your problems will seem. They won't be so great, or so big. They won't consume you if you rise above them. While you're dwelling in your problems, while you are amongst them, while you are putting your focus on them, they will consume you. Your perception of them will be off. You won't be able to hear God clearly. You won't be focused. Elevate your mind! Elevate yourself! When a feeling of defeat tries to creep in, remind yourself to elevate your mind and change your focus. We are focused on the wrong thing if we are unhappy. We all go through tough times; it's inevitable. Since you have to go through it, choose how you do it.

There will be circumstances that will make us sad, and we will deal with trauma after life-altering challenges. Hard times will come. Unbelievable and unimaginable situations may occur. Things will knock you right off your feet. Your faith will be tested. Wilderness experiences will happen. There may be times when you feel that God is no longer by your side. You may feel as if He has left you and allowed things in your life that you think you are not ready to deal with. You may get to the point where you question if He is even real.

THE HARDEST POINT IN MY LIFE

On December 16, 2015, my mother called me. I could hear something different in her voice. I knew that she was scheduled to go to the doctor that day, but I believed God and trusted Him to answer my prayer concerning the problem that was occurring in her body. So, when she called, I sat and listened in disbelief. "Mesey, I'm at the doctor and they're getting ready to give me a biopsy. They gave me a mammogram and they found a lump." (Paraphrased quote) She also asked me to pray. The tears began to well up in my eyes. I thought to myself, *God no! Please God! I've already lost my father to this horrific disease. God, not my mother too. Please God don't let this thing be.* I remember that moment so vividly because it was so intense. I googled her symptoms and prayed against cancer days and weeks before this time. I didn't just say a prayer. I puh-rayed. I snotted. I cried. I pled the blood of Jesus.

I still trusted Him to let the "lump" be gone before the medical staff could even perform the biopsy. I trusted Him to dry it up in that moment. I believed and still believe that if He just spoke the word, it wouldn't be there. She hung up the phone. The silence rang in my ears as I thought to myself, *What now?* I remember calling my brother and telling him what happened. We spoke briefly, and my mother called me right back. I answered the phone, and she began to apologize. She told me that she was sorry for calling and dumping that news in my lap like she did. She said that she just wanted me to pray. I can't remember if I prayed on the phone with her or after we hung up, but I expressed to Mom that there was no need to apologize. I assured her that I understood and that it was okay.

Being the absolute best mother that she was, she briefed me on what she was doing, where she was, how nice the staff was, and how one specific doctor came over to the hospital to be with her during this procedure since she was alone. A nurse had given her a graham cracker or some small snack since she was hungry and hadn't eaten (she hadn't anticipated being gone so long). I sat and listened to her while fighting to hold my emotions inside. Satan whispered in my ear, "You lost your father to cancer and now you will lose your mother the same way." I had to elevate my mind above the situation, or I would have temporarily lost it.

As we awaited the results of the biopsy, my mother, brother, and sister drove from Ohio to North Carolina to visit me. During that visit, I could see the pain my mother was in. It hurt my heart to see her like that. One particular day, we decided to do some Christmas shopping at the mall. Now my mother had never been one to not want to walk the mall and shop, but in the middle of shopping, she was ready to leave. She needed to rest. Also, during that visit, she couldn't sleep in a bed. Her swollen arm and hand made it impossible for her to get comfortable laying down. Thankfully, she could get comfortable on the chaise connected to my sectional.

One night, I couldn't sleep, so I quietly went out to the living room, sat on the ottoman in front of the sectional, and I just stared at her while she slept sitting up. The living room was dimly lit with the glow from the television, which was pretty much muted per her request, and by the illuminated streetlights outside the window. I began to pray within myself. I gazed upon her beauty, reflected on the part of her life that I was blessed to have with her, and with a grateful heart, thanked God for her life. As I sat there, she opened her eyes, subtly startled because she didn't expect anyone to be right in front of her; she smiled at me. She asked me how long I had been sitting there, what I was doing, and we just had a conversation. I look back and I cherish that time.

Shortly after my family went back to Ohio, we received the diagnosis. We were faced with Stage 4 Triple Negative Breast Cancer that could not be operated on. Various hormone treatments were not options. Chemotherapy and radiation were the options taken. At the very end of February 2016, I flew to Ohio for a few days to help Mom. While there, I learned that chemotherapy had done nothing.

Towards the close of March 2016, my husband, children, and I drove to Ohio for Spring break and to help Mom. I could see the drastic decline in her health even though I was just there a little over three weeks prior. At the end of that visit, it was terribly hard for me to leave. I didn't know if that was the last time I would see her alive. I didn't know if I should tell her goodbye. The uncertainties swirled through my mind without retreat. As soon as I walked in the door to my home in North Carolina, I was informed that my mother had to be hospitalized.

I didn't know if I would have to turn around and drive back to Ohio, but what I did know, is that

I wanted to be with her. I prayed and I asked my Heavenly Father to allow me to be with my mother when she transitioned if He wasn't going to heal her on the earth. Mom was in the hospital for a few days and came home for palliative care. I stayed in touch with my siblings, and they kept me updated about the situation. I wished I could be there every day. My brother and sister did an outstanding job of taking care of my mother.

On April 19, 2016, I received a call from the nurse telling me that Mom had hours to days to live and that I should come. In that same afternoon, I tidied up the house a bit, did laundry, packed my bags, booked my flight (It was $30.00 by the way. God did it!), picked my children up from school, braided my daughter's hair, and made sure that everything was set for them. My husband took emergency vacation to accommodate the situation at hand (my sister-in-law was on standby for me, and a few days later, she came all the way from Ohio with her mother and son in tow to take care of my children). I was still a little unsure of how everything was going to pan out, but I was for sure that God was answering my prayer. I was on my flight that evening and arrived in Ohio that night. Once I got to Mom's bedside, I felt better. Grateful that God answered my prayer, I sat and stared at her while she slept. I wasn't going anywhere. I was right there with her. I was with my best friend until the end.

Early Wednesday morning, April 27, 2016, I woke up because Mom's breathing changed. I remained in the chair, fully reclined, just listening and looking through the rails of the provided hospice bed. I watched as her chest rose and dropped. It rose; it dropped. It rose; it dropped...... I sat there timing the seconds between each breath. One particular stretch of time made me get up. I rushed to her side, rubbed the side of her head, and comforted her in any way I could. I alerted my aunt in the next room that her breathing wasn't right. I asked if she would go get my brother from another part of the house. Meanwhile, her chest rose, and it dropped. It rose; it dropped. Seconds kept going by, time kept moving, and I sat there waiting for Mom to breathe again. I watched and watched. I waited and waited...........Nothing. She was gone.

Even though time continued to tick by, my world stopped. *Is she really gone? Just wait for*

Ronnie. I stared at her and kept rubbing her face or her hand in disbelief. *Did that really just happen?* I heard my aunt and brother coming down the hallway. I looked up and my brother asked me if she had passed. I just looked at him. It was hard for me to answer him. I knew she was gone, but it was hard for me to say it. I told them how many seconds it had been since she took her last breath. *I have to call my sister. I have to call my husband. I have to make several calls. I have to make sure no one tells the children before I can get back to North Carolina to tell them myself.* Those seconds kept going, but my world was at a standstill. I was moving and taking care of necessary business, making calls, answering the door when loved ones came to be with us and see Mom one more time, but my world had completely halted. The nurse was called to officially declare Mom dead. Her medications were properly disposed of. I made the call to the funeral director.

Stewart and Calhoun's funeral home staff came to get Mom. As they wheeled the gurney through the living room towards the front door, her face exposed as the body bag was not fully zipped, you could hear the sniffles and feel the monstrosity of heaviness due to our great loss. I asked the staff if I could kiss her one final time before they took her from the home she created and dwelled in the previous 47 years.

Tick. Tock. Time kept moving. My world was completely still. In these moments, we (my brother, my sister, and myself) were business minded. We made funeral arrangements and took care of business. We did what was necessary to do in the time of a loved one's death. We kept going. Within the next week and a half, I flew home to North Carolina, packed everyone up, and drove back to Ohio, gathered with family and friends, ate lots of fried chicken, reminisced on the good times, ran errands, went to the funeral home to do Mom's hair before the final family viewing, and finally, proceeded to her funeral on May 7, 2016--the day before Mother's Day.

Life, around me, went on. The day after her funeral, family and friends around me celebrated their mothers and I plastered a smile on my face all the while, so very empty inside. I was surrounded by all this love, but the void was there stealing my happiness for the moment. No, I was not happy. In fact, I was more than not happy. I was angry! I was disappointed and hurt. Depression rose up, but yet I smiled.

Family and friends went back to their respective homes. My husband, our children, and I returned to North Carolina. My children went back to school. My husband went back to work. The world kept going 'round, but not mine. It stopped back on April 27th at approximately 3:12 in the morning. Yes, we were well into May now. Yes, Mom was now at rest with God. Yes, she was in no more pain. Yes, sir. Yes, ma'am. I believe to be absent from the body is to be present with the Lord, BUT THIS HURTS!!! I just kept moving. I stayed busy. Yes, I cried. Yes, I knew I was grieving. Yes, I knew I could pray, and God was the ultimate comforter. Yes, yes. I knew.

During those quiet moments (they were rare for me at this time), Satan would speak to me, "I told you!" "God didn't hear you about your father OR your mother." "Why do you even pray?" "God doesn't hear you!" He came for me y'all! Like, he came for me HARD. Instead of turning to the Scriptures and praying, I started to listen. He would say things like, "What good does praying do anyway?" "You lost both your parents even though you and others prayed so hard for them." "God is going to do what he wants to do anyway, so why even pray?!" The more I listened, the more depressed I grew. It was at that point that I began to give control of my thoughts over to Satan.

As time passed by, I grew angrier at my husband because I felt like he wasn't there for me. There was this huge emotional disconnect the entire bout of my mother's sickness. I was so mad! He didn't understand me or what I was going through. He would go to work, come home, sleep and do it all over again, but my world had stopped. I wondered if he even knew that I was hurting so badly. I thought to myself that he hadn't lost either of his parents; he still had both of his grandmothers, so I wanted to give him the benefit of the doubt because he didn't understand. Just as quickly as those ideas came to mind, I would try to push them out because he was my husband, and surely, he had to know I was hurting. I had just lost my mother. My rock. My A1. The very person who birthed me. *Why would he not know?! Why was he not talking to me about it and telling me he's in my corner?! How could he be so insensitive?!* The notion of him not being there for me ate at me and gave Satan more territory to work in. I just gave him more and more control. No, I didn't want to read the Word, and no, I was not going to pray. Why would I? Instead, I am going to leave North Carolina and go to Ohio to get away from this man who doesn't understand me or even care to.

So, I left. School had just let out for the summer, so I packed mine and my children's bags and left. I had no idea when or if I was going to go back. I just knew that I needed to be around my brother and sister because they understood the pain I was bearing. We were all bearing that same motherless pain. There was work to be done at Mom's house. So, I packed up her "First Lady" hats, her clothes, her shoes, other belongings and so on. I went through drawers and closets. I went through stuff. I threw things away. I donated items to the Goodwill. I just kept moving.

One day, I went to lunch with my dear mentor friend, my doula who was at my side with child number three. She told me how good I looked. I smiled and was glad that my outside didn't match my inside. Further into our lunch, she asked me how I was really doing. I couldn't lie. She knew I wasn't good. I looked good, but I wasn't good. She had also suffered the loss of her mother years prior. I opened up to her about most everything. She asked me if I had been in my Word. (She already knew the answer to that, I'm convinced.) I told her, "No." We spoke for quite a while, I expressed myself, and she told me to get back into my Word. She urged me to read three times more than before. She sat there and ministered to me in such a loving way. I knew that I needed to hear it, but I didn't want to because I was angry and felt like God didn't hear my prayers. She told me that with all the chaos that was going on in my life, with everything going on in my world, I needed to remind myself of who God was. She told me that He is still Holy; He is still righteous; He is still faithful. She just flat out ministered to me. I took a hold of what she said, but I still chose to continue to wallow in grief the wrong way. I was choosing how I did it. I continued to let Satan have control.

As more days passed, I barely spoke to my husband. He didn't understand what I was going through and I just wanted him to stay far away from me. We spoke briefly when he would call, and his concern caused him to ask me when I was coming back home. I would tell him that I didn't know. I tried to find ways to numb the pain I was going through, but nothing helped. Cleaning out her closet didn't help. Going through her things didn't help. Shutting my husband out of my life seemed to help at the time, but ultimately it didn't help. And since I was desperate to feel better, I turned to alcohol. But guess what, alcohol didn't help.

After almost a month of this travesty, my husband and I began to explore the option of divorce. (Insert Big Eyes emoji here.) Yes, it was a brief exploration, but the disconnection was so great. Satan was probably watching and rubbing his hands together, waiting in excitement as this all unfolded. The day after this conversation, my husband flew up to Ohio to surprise me. I remember sitting in a restaurant with my father-in-law, my children, my brother, my sister, and my brand-new baby niece. My husband called my phone and asked what I was doing. I responded that I was having dinner at Cracker Barrel, etc. I had no idea that he was in town and not far from me. Before I knew it, my daughter yelled, "Daddy!" I said, "Your daddy is in..." and then I looked up.

I have to say, when I saw him walk into that restaurant, my heart dropped and I thought to myself, *Why is he here?* I was disappointed and didn't feel like dealing with him. Once he sat down, tension was present at the table, and I tried so hard to mask my true feelings. *Here this man is invading my space. I drove eight and a half hours for this space and here he is in it.*

After we left the restaurant, he asked if we could go out later that evening to talk. I didn't want to talk. I didn't even want him there, but I agreed. On the way to the park where we would talk, I asked him to swing me by the Flagpole. The Flagpole is a liquor drive thru in Akron, Ohio. He was super confused and hesitated, but tensions were already thick, so he just went. If I was going to be around him and actually endure *this* difficult conversation, I wanted to make sure that I had an attempt at numbing myself. During that conversation, I opened up so much about my feelings. In the midst of talking, I drank, and I drank. I drank more than I ever had in my entire life. I have never been "a drinker", but that stretch after my rock passed, was more than difficult. I cried and just let it all out. I told my husband everything. He apologized for not being there. He told me that hindsight was 20/20 and that he could see now where he was not there for me. We had one of the best conversations to date, me being drunk and all.

The next morning, I thoroughly paid for the previous night. I told God that I would not ever do that again if He would just help me make it through. It was my first and last hangover at the age of 32. So, there I was, praying to the Lord in my drunkenness, and I have not stopped praying since!

STARTING TO HEAL

When I returned back to North Carolina, a couple days after my husband did, I applied the strategies of my dear mentor friend. I got back in my Word and God was right there! He spoke to me like never before and I felt so much better. I made sure that I was reading three times per day-- morning, a midday pick-me-up, and before bed. The pain didn't fully subside, but it became so much more bearable. I knew that God hadn't left me. I knew that God was always there. I turned my back on him and allowed Satan to have his way in my life. I went through a wilderness experience. In that wilderness, I questioned God's existence. I just knew that if He did exist, He didn't hear me, and He hadn't heard me. I was in a deep, dark place for a little while, but I found my way back to Him. He was there with open arms. At that time, my world continued. I say to you at this time, don't allow your feelings to make you forsake your faith!

I shared this very personal experience because it's so important for us to **remember who God is** and to **elevate ourselves above our problems** even if they are utterly devastating. There is nothing wrong with grieving because it is necessary and it is a process, but it becomes unhealthy when we wallow in it. When we allow grief to control us, we are wrong. When we put our grief before God in our lives, we are wrong. Grief then becomes our idol. Instead of wallowing in my grief and allowing Satan to speak to my mind, I should have drawn closer to Him. It didn't just happen overnight though. There was a period in which I felt so disconnected from God even before Mom passed. Her short illness and untimely death were the icing on the cake.

That was when the devil turned up the heat and he thought he had me. He will come for you just like he came for me. And he will keep coming and coming. He is resilient! We must "Be alert and of sober mind. Your enemy the devil prowls around like a roaring lion looking for someone to devour." (I Peter 5:8 NIV) In other words, be aware of the sins that pull you and the temptations that attempt to pull you away from God and His call on your life. Satan wants to destroy you. He wants you to think that you're good where you are. He wants you to be mediocre and not live your life to the fullest. Don't allow him to do it!

For those who feel that ridding their lives of God is a solution, think again. I recently heard Dr. Tony Evans say, "If you get rid of God, you still have your problem." These words resonated with me. Upon hearing, I repeated them in my head. At the time when I needed God the most (always but especially in this difficult time), I attempted to forget Him. Even though I gave up on prayer and reading the Word, my grief and pain was still very present. I was angry and disappointed that He would allow this to happen. In all my anger, my problem was still there.

I could look back and say that I regret having gone through that, but the fact of the matter is, I do not. If I hadn't gone through it, I wouldn't have been able to share that experience with you. I prayed and asked God to allow what I went through to help someone know or even remember that He is ALWAYS there! When bad things happen, He is still there. Take the opportunity to get closer to Him during those tough times.

THE POINT OF IT ALL

The last key point of this chapter that I would like to talk about is the most important. **Cultivate (or begin if you don't have one) your relationship with God and develop a prayer life!** This is the most important way that I live my life to the fullest. The Bible tells us, "But seek first his kingdom and his righteousness, and all these things will be given to you as well." (Matthew 6:33 NIV) It is so easy to become wrapped up in the cares of this world, to be consumed with materialistic things, and to succumb to a busy or hectic everyday lifestyle. We should be aware of these distractions and put forth a conscious effort to keep God first in our lives. I am reminded of a message that my father preached years ago entitled "The Main Thing is to Keep the Main Thing the Main Thing." This title is pretty self-explanatory. Keep God FIRST, numero uno, alpha...and EVERYTHING else will fall in line. How can you do this? I'm glad you asked. It's called RELATIONSHIP.

Did you know that God desires to have a relationship and fellowship with you? He does! With you! YES, YOU! Yes, me! And I am so grateful! In order for there to be relationship, there has to be relations. Relations are connections. You see, God is always connected to us. This connection will remain singular unless reciprocity occurs. I don't want God to be connected to me and I am not connected to Him. God has already done His part, and He is always there with His hand stretched towards you. God is with you, but ARE YOU WITH HIM? Have you tapped into the source of your strength? Have you plugged yourself in? How can we have POWER if we are not plugged in and if we haven't made the connection? Don't live beneath your privilege. Don't allow anyone or anything to stop you from connecting and staying connected to HIM. If you once had that connection and you allowed Satan, through whatever vehicle, to aid in you breaking the connection, fight and PLUG BACK IN! There is safety in CONNECTION.

A very popular song (which originated as a poem) comes to mind. "What a Friend We Have in Jesus," coined in 1855 by Joseph M. Scriven, an Irish poet, is made up of life-changing lyrics:

What a Friend we have in Jesus,
All our sins and griefs to bear!
What a privilege to carry
Everything to God in prayer!
O what peace we often forfeit,
O what needless pain we bear,
All because we do not carry
Everything to God in prayer!

Have we trials and temptations?
Is there trouble anywhere?
We should never be discouraged,
Take it to the Lord in prayer.

Can we find a friend so faithful
Who will all our sorrows share?
Jesus knows our every weakness,
Take it to the Lord in prayer.

Are we weak and heavy-laden,

Cumbered with a load of care?

Precious Savior, still our refuge—

Take it to the Lord in prayer;

Do thy friends despise, forsake thee?

Take it to the Lord in prayer;

In His arms He'll take and shield thee,

Thou wilt find a solace there.

The story behind these lyrics is a truly powerful one. In your free time, I encourage you to read about it, review them slowly, and realize just what you have--just what you have been given. Connect! Tap in! Stay connected!

Jesus is our friend, and many are living beneath their privilege of even knowing Him. We have the privilege of taking everything to Him in prayer. Prayer is communication with God. It is a two-way street. Many times, I speak with my eldest son about communication. The example that I give him is about the relationship that he and I have. I asked him if I get up every morning, get ready for my day, walk past him and say nothing, go about my daily routine without even acknowledging him, and finally lay down to sleep at night without having said anything to him, how would that make him feel? Now on occasion, I've told him that I loved him, but my daily routine doesn't back up that proclamation. He told me that it wouldn't feel good at all. My words and my actions would conflict. He would be confused about if I actually meant what I said. We can say we love God, but if our actions aren't matching our proclamation, then do we really? If we get up, eat breakfast, lunch, dinner, snack or whatever (that He provided), breathe air (that is His) enjoy (or not) a day (that He has made and given), but we don't ever stop and communicate with Him (or maybe we do once a week during worship service on Sunday), do we love Him for real?

Since prayer is a two-way street, it is imperative that both parts be fulfilled in order to be effective. Prayer is not an opportunity to drop off your shopping list to God of what you want. It's so much more than that. Prayer is us talking to our Creator, the King of Kings, and the Lord of Lords. It is also, us LISTENING! Yes, we must not only *say*, but we must also listen for Him to *relay*.

There are two books that I urge you to read. Both of them analyze communication with God.

The first one is *How to Listen to God* by Charles Stanley. I can't even describe what reading this book has done for me. The second book was written by a friend of mine, Dr. Matisa Wilbon. This life-changing book entitled, #*Undefeated: Prayer Never Loses* says, "Prayer is the umbilical cord that provides the spiritual sustenance needed between life and its source." Both of these books provide in-depth details that could help you if you wanted to be helped and change you if you want to be changed.

As this chapter closes, I pray that something has sparked in you to begin or continue living your life to the fullest. If you feel unfulfilled, you don't have to. Remember that you have the power to change. God, please give us the courage to change the things we can.

Living Your Dash to the Fullest
Points to Ponder

———

1. Engage in **physical exercise** daily.

2. **Exercise your mentality** (practice self-control and self-discipline) and **embrace change**.

3. **Establish a routine** (practice positivity).

4. **Always be grateful and go after dreams.**

5. **Elevate yourself above your problems** (draw close to God) and **remember who God is**.

6. **Cultivate** (begin, if needed) **a relationship with God** and **develop your prayer life**.

Chapter Three
Living My Dash Like It's Golden

————

It *is* golden! It is precious, and it is a gift! We have to be very careful how we treat ourselves. We need to make sure that we unconditionally love on ourselves and continue to build ourselves up. We have to be proud of who we are, our accomplishments, learn from our mistakes and keep going.

One day, I felt compelled to ask three of my four children (my 5-year-old wanted nothing to do with the conversation) what it means to live your life like it's golden. Two of the accounts were very similar. After telling me that they didn't know (because they wanted to do something more "important") they said, (in no particular order) "Make it yours. Make it good. Have a good life. Do good. Be good. Be nice. Be kind. Be grateful. Be loving. Be respectful." My 13-year-old took it a bit further. He said, "Golden stuff costs a lot and you wanna take care of stuff that costs a lot because it's valuable."

With a little more prodding, he continued, "Live your life like it's valuable, like it's something and take care of it or something." He walked off. I sat there and reflected on what he said. Then I looked at the notes I took while he was speaking. This spoke volumes to me because I love the way he thinks and because so many of us (young, middle aged, and seasoned) don't treat our dashes like they're valuable. After a short while, he came back to add, "Gold is rare and special just like life. Gold in its purest form is hard to find." Then he walked off and left me sitting there, pondering his words. There were so many thoughts that developed in my mind regarding his simile. Take from it what you wish, but let's focus on the word **valuable**.

WORTH

Valuable (adj.): worth a price. (Merriam-Webster) When something is valuable, it's worth something. Your life is valuable; it is worth something! Do you know your worth? Do you know whose you are? If you don't, let me school you. If you do, let me remind you.

Many years ago, my father told a story (I'm going to paraphrase it) about a little boy who hand crafted a small toy boat. He took his time and effort to perfect the boat just as he wanted. It was one of a kind. One day, he took it to the creek (or as Dad would say, "the crick") to play with it on the water. As he was enjoying the little boat that he loved so much, the water began to carry it down the creek; the little boy lost it. He was overcome with sadness because he placed great value in his creation. It was now gone. Some days later, he went to town with his mother. While out, he ran into another little boy who was playing with **his** toy boat. Hopeful, he went up to the boy and told him what happened. Because the other little boy was unwilling to part with the boat, the creator offered to pay to get it back. It worked! Elated that he had gotten his boat back, the little boy looked at it and said, "You're mine twice. I made you, and now I bought you back!"

You see, this story is one of my favorites that Dad told while preaching. It describes the perfect love. God made us. Satan deceived us. We fell and were lost, but Jesus paid the ultimate price to get us back! **The greatest love of all!** You are worth so much, that God gave His one and only Son to die for you. Yes, you are to die for! "For God so loved the world that he gave his one and only Son, that whoever believes in him shall not perish but have eternal life." (John 3:16 NIV) God made us and He bought us back! We were bought at a price. The ultimate sacrifice was made for us. No one or nothing can separate us from the love of God. No matter what someone has told you, no matter where you are in your life right now, no matter how much you may or may not have messed up, no matter what you think about yourself, YOU ARE LOVED, VALUABLE and WORTH celebrating!

CELEBRATE

So many times, we are slow to celebrate ourselves. We can truly be our own worst critic. We will beat ourselves up over a mistake, a fall, or a small failure, but when we have a victory, be it large or small, we, more times than none, downplay it and don't celebrate it. Listen! Celebrate yourself! Be who you are and celebrate you! Celebrate your accomplishments, reaching your goals whether large or small, and making it through another day. You may think to yourself that the latter is trivial. But guess what, it is not. Making it through another day is an accomplishment, especially if you have lived your life to the fullest during that day. These are victories that deserve to be applauded. There will be people, family even, who we think are for us, celebrating us out in the open but secretly wanting to see us fail. Jealousy is ugly and it will show itself in the most subtle ways through those who may be closest to us. The older I get, the more this becomes apparent.

You will miss opportunities to rejoice in your small victories if you're always waiting for big things to happen or for others to do the celebrating for you. "They" may not ever celebrate you. Do you continue to wait? No! Look at yourself in the mirror and as weird as it may feel, tell yourself how proud you are of you. You will always have those who speak negatively about and to you. You don't need to do it to yourself too. Speak positively about yourself to yourself. Remember who and whose you are!

If you feel as though you have nothing to celebrate, start opening your eyes and look around you. If you don't like what you see, start changing what you see. Work towards your goals. Rewrite your narrative. You have the power to do this. You owe it to yourself and others to go after what's in your heart. You owe it to yourself and others to be who you are called to be and to do what you're called to do. Someone is waiting to hear your story. Someone needs you to pour love into them. Someone is waiting for you to walk in your destiny for them.

IT'S NOT EVEN ABOUT YOU

Many times, we don't realize that what we have experienced or have encountered isn't even about us. When we face adversities of whatever kind, we will always have a testimony after going through them. You didn't face and defeat those giants in your life just to say that you did. They built your strength, character, perseverance, and the list goes on. "...because you know that the testing of your faith produces perseverance." (James 1:3 NIV) Aside from what they did for and in you, you now have a testimony that will help and encourage someone else. You can witness to them about what you did to get through. Back in Chapter 2, I shared with you my testimony and the experience I went through when my mother died. That wasn't just for me to keep to myself; it was for whoever needed to hear it. Your testimony will encourage and build others up. It will serve as confirmation for those needing it. Your testimony is golden! It's precious! Your dash is golden; it's valuable and, it's also meant to be shared with others.

WHO'S IN YOUR CIRCLE?

Who you have in your circle is of the utmost importance. Because your dash is golden, you cannot let everyone in. One day, I was watching Red Table Talk. Willow Smith said something that was so insightful about bringing people (or a potential significant other) to meet her parents. She, so eloquently said, "I know for me, wherever my parents are is a sacred space..." "...that person may not be able to hold the importance of that space." Just like Willow and many young people with similar outlooks who don't bring some people around their parents, we should be aware and selective as to whom we allow in the sacred space of our lives. That sacred space, that golden space is priceless.

Once we allow someone in our space, we also have to be able to decipher whether they are in our dashes for a reason, for a season, or for a lifetime.

When someone is in your life for a reason, it may be to help you through a difficult time, challenge you to grow your patience and strength, or for any other reason. The thing is, when that need has been met, there will come a time when you have to let go of them. Or if you are that friend, it's time for you to move on. This doesn't mean you are enemies or that you don't get along or even talk, but that person should no longer be in your circle.

Those who are in your life for a season are not permanent fixtures either. They are there for an extended amount of time but are not meant to be there for life. As a teen, I had a group of friends with whom I spent my weekends, free time, and the like. We hung tough, whether it was all together or just a few of us at a time. We were there for each other, cried and prayed with each other, celebrated one another, and went through the good, the bad, and the ugly together. They were my girls who felt more like sisters. After a couple years of having this reciprocal support system of sisterhood, we began to grow apart. Some of us got married while others of us remained single. Life began to take us in different directions. At the time, I didn't understand how we could be so close and then over the course of a few short months, not be. I struggled to get over life bringing about this change.

Throughout the course of some time, I believe I went through the grief and loss stages. My loss was losing my girls (some of them). Only looking back do I recognize this. At some point or another, I was in denial about us beginning to grow apart. The signs and circumstances were there, but I didn't want to accept it. I became angry at them and myself for how things happened. I was angry because I was losing those who were, besides my family, closest to me. This made me sad. I may have bounced back and forth between anger and depression.

As time went on, I found some peace concerning the situation. When it came to having people in my life, I accepted this motto for myself: People come, and people go. This is how I was able to accept losing my girls. I had to accept that they were seasonal friends. They were in my life for a season. When that season was over, I had to let go. Don't get me wrong, I don't hate them at all. I still love them, and I know they love me too. To this day, there may be a text or phone exchange, a rare lunch or dinner date, or an even rarer gathering between us and we will have a great time. However, it will never be like it once was. In fact, it wasn't even all of the girls who parted ways. Some of us were closer than others of us and it is okay. Life happens. We grow up and we may grow apart. Life has us in different places. If you have seasonal friends, accept it when the season of your friendship is over.

Lastly, there will be people in your life who are there for a lifetime. This type of friend is truly rare. The two of you can tell each other when either is wrong with love and in turn, it is accepted with love. You all remain friends, learn from each other throughout your lives, and are in it for the long haul. These friends are there with you through the reasons and seasons. The physical distance between you will never matter. I have a handful of lifetime friends. I cherish these people with my life. We know how we feel about each other, and there is no question about it. We can go without conversing for weeks or months even, but we will pick up right where we left off without missing a beat when we do.

God gave me one particular friend, whom I learned early on was a lifetime friend, when I was 27 years old. I met her at work and not long after I met her, God gave me a dream concerning her. When I had this dream, I didn't know if it was God who gave it or if it was the dinner I ate the previous evening. Despite this, one day, I went to her after work to tell her about my dream. On my way to her office, various questions came to my mind: *Was she a believer? Was she married? Was she a kind person?* and the list went on. When I made it to her office, I was timid because of the uncertainty. I just said something pretty general to begin, but in a quick few moments, I felt like I knew her. I still didn't know anything about her, but as the conversation went on (for quite some time) I knew from the God love I felt that we made a connection.

It was no ordinary connection, and it would be there for the rest of our lives. God brought us together. I am so grateful for her and my handful of lifetime friends. I am also grateful for the reason and season friends as well. Each type of friend that we have is significant and plays important roles in our lives. Don't regret having each type of friend because they are all placed in our lives according to God's plan. In addition, we must remember that we may also be someone's reason, season, or lifetime friend. When they let you go, go!

Though we have friends, acquaintances, family and loved ones, we shouldn't rely on them to validate us. Never seek your validation from another human being. If someone has to validate you, you will always seek to please others, and "others" collectively will never be pleased. Only seek validation from God. That is when you will begin to walk in your purpose.

TAKE IT ONE DAY AT A TIME: WHAT IS BALANCE?

Take each day one at a time. After all, that's how they come. "Therefore, do not worry about tomorrow, for tomorrow will worry about itself." (Matthew 6:34 NIV) Of course this scripture isn't telling us to not plan or be prepared; that would be contradictory. What it is saying is that we shouldn't be wrapped up in or become overwhelmed in worry about the days ahead. God knows the way that we take. All we have to do is walk in His perfect plan for our lives, doing it one day at a time.

In each day, self-care is imperative. If you don't take care of yourself, who will? You cannot pour from an empty cup. Whether it's taking that 30-minute nap, getting a quick massage, reading a book that will help you, jumping on the elliptical, or meditating, take care of yourself. Take that vacation. I once had someone tell me that vacations are fantasies; they are not your reality. I had to disagree with this because when you are on vacation, there in those moments, they are your reality. They are your now. Live in it and enjoy it!

I believe another form of self-care is having some type of balance. But what is balance? At times, I think we feel that our lives should be perfectly balanced, but they will never be perfectly balanced. We will add unnecessary stress trying to perfect our balance.

During the summer months, I tend to overthink my children's schedules. I feel like I have to continually push them each minute of each day to read, do math, practice typing skills, and have a perfectly balanced summer life to prepare them for returning to school in the Fall. The thing is, I am only one person, and they are four people at different ages and in different stages of their dashes and development. Trying to juggle four different curriculums, six different personalities (theirs, mine, and my husband's), while remaining sane is not something for which I am good. In fact, I'm so not good at it that I don't even do it anymore. I was wrapped up in perfecting balance that it was too stressful and non-beneficial for everyone involved. I'm sure my children would agree. So now, I realize that the balance won't be perfect and it's difficult for me to follow a strict agenda with four children. I no longer wanted to lose myself in trying to have it "perfect" based on something other than MY reality.

You see, we create a picture in our minds (or society paints one for us) of what balance looks like. Who says what it looks like? We will kill ourselves trying to be perfect. Be okay with not being perfect because the reality of it is, we're not and will never, ever be. Guess what? No one else is or will be either! Whew! Take the pressure off your shoulders. At the same time, don't use this as a cop out. Don't use the excuse of not being perfect to excuse laziness, lack of self-discipline, or unattractive behavior. You're better than that!

GET HELP! DON'T STRUGGLE!

Hey! Your dash is too precious to struggle in silence. Mine is too. For this very reason, while I was in the middle of finishing this book, I took myself to therapy. When you live your dash like it's golden, you care enough about yourself to get necessary help. That does not mean you're crazy, you're weak, or that you even have such great deficits in your dash. However, it does mean that you recognize the challenge and chose to attack it.

Back in Chapter 1, I briefly spoke about seeking help when needed. After I wrote that, I made plans to go myself. I wanted to make sure that I actually did what I was encouraging others to do. I knew that I had suffered the loss of both my parents: I lost my father almost 14 years ago and my mother almost three years ago. I was also aware of the dark place I was in after my mother's death. I knew that I was traumatized as a result of both of their deaths, so I wanted to make sure that I had gone through the grief and loss process in a healthy manner.

Lastly, I felt that something was just "off" with me. I felt overwhelmed and underwhelmed at the same time. I'm not even sure if that makes sense, but it's how I felt. Looking back, I discovered that I had lost control of my thoughts again. Not nearly as bad as after my mother passed away, but I was lost in the wife, mommy, nurse, doctor, referee, coach, cheerleader, amongst all these other roles. There was homework help needed, breakfast, lunch and dinner to be packed and made, conversations about my husband's job and life were had, quality time spent, grocery store runs made, walls of laundry to be done, toilets to be cleaned, spills to be wiped, hugs and kisses to be given and received, and the list goes on. I had forgotten about me so much until I began to identify with someone I wasn't. Where was I? Where was Mariesa? How do I get her back?

Therapy/counseling quickly helped me put the pieces back together. Lightbulbs, as my God-ordained therapist says, turned on and I began to see things much more clearly. My peace was preserved. I was reintroduced to MYSELF! I loved ME so much and to the point where I didn't care what it looked like, I was going to improve me. My requirement for myself was to become a happier, healthier and whole me. As a result, I am a happier, healthier and whole wife, mother, sister, friend, and most importantly, servant of God. God not only wants your whole heart, He also wants your heart whole.

I want you happier, healthier, and whole. If you are, I want you to stay that way. The thing is, for a long time, I thought I was just fine too. Yes, I had struggles, but who doesn't? I knew God heard my prayers so I would just keep on praying. There is NOTHING too hard for Him. Even though all of this is factual, I needed additional help to renew my mind in a different way. If you've ever dealt with the loss of a parent, a child or any other loved one, seeking counsel could be most beneficial. You'd be surprised how much counseling can help you with daily life in general. Therapy helps you put the pieces of life's puzzle back together again. Because your dash is golden, take the time to put the pieces back together again. You deserve to be happier, healthier, and whole...a complete puzzle, God's Masterpiece.

Chapter Four
My Dash Matters

———

Someone once told me that people will hold you to a higher standard than they hold themselves. The more I thought on it, the truer it became to me. Folks will take your past and count it as your now and your future all while turning a blind eye to their own past and mess. Don't be a victim of this bondage. Break free from the chains of opinions, scrutiny, people and the past. Grant yourself grace for those things that have already happened and move forward.

Occasionally, I have heard people say, "Only God can judge me," but just know that people can, and they do judge you. They won't stop. The beauty of it is that what "they" say doesn't matter. What He says about you is the only factor that counts.

NON-FACTORS

When my children come to me with something someone has said to them at school that was mean, I will ask them a question or two, but first I remind them of who they are, and I reinforce who the offender is. The conversation may go a little something like this: "Mom, Maria kept calling me ugly today." "Did you let the teacher know?" "Yes ma'am." "Are you ugly?" "No." "That's right! Where are you beautiful?" "Inside and out." "Exactly! Don't ever allow anyone, I don't care who it is, tell you anything different! You are smart, kind, and important. Usually when people have something negative to say about you, they're insecure within themselves. Remember that there's nothing wrong with you; there's something going wrong for them. They are non-factors."

I teach my children to be kind, but not to be doormats. You must have tough skin when dealing with the world. A person who I say is a non-factor is someone who doesn't add to your life in a positive way but rather attempts to tear you down to their level. You don't have to be around them all the time, and they are not in your circle. They are a non-factor. Be kind to them, show them love, but you don't have to be a doormat or be around their negativity, especially when it's directed at you. Non factor's opinions don't matter, but they will suck the life out of you if you allow it. Stay away from people like that. This goes across the board for children, adults, and the seasoned adults.

I have encountered many people who have had their opinions about me. You have too. The thing is, what people say about me is not my business. What people say about you is not your business. Do you know what *is* your business? What God says about you. That is your business. Focus on Him and that. If you focus on pleasing God, you will never go wrong. If you focus on whom He called you to be, you will be at peace.

We should strive for peace to the point where we are okay with walking away from anyone and everything who/that is working against peace in our lives. The older I get, the easier it is for me to accept the fact that everyone is not made to be in my circle nor I in theirs. In middle and high school, I would find myself wondering why I didn't fit in with the "popular" girls. I learned to ignore the nasty comments some made about the way I dressed or about why my hair was always in the same ponytail. At the time, I lacked self-confidence and felt like I needed to fit in to be accepted.

FIT IN? WHAT'S FITTING IN?

Trying to fit in with everyone is a sign of immaturity. My middle and high school self hadn't yet matured and grown to be strong and comfortable with who I was. I was not yet fully aware of my worth. When you know your worth, when you know who and whose you are, when you are good in the skin you're in, you won't worry about fitting in with any and everyone else. Remember what my son said in the last chapter? He said, "gold, in its purest form, is rare." You are rare! You will not fit in with everyone. You will outgrow people. Many won't understand you, but that's okay. Be okay with that.

What really matters is that the God of all gods, the King of Glory, the Creator of Heaven and Earth understands you. You fit in perfectly with Him always. However, He strategically puts some people in our lives to remind us of His love and for human companionship. He blesses us with friends and family with whom we can share our lives. He hears you and inclines His ear to you. He knows exactly who/what you need and when you need them/it. Do you know what a privilege it is to walk with Him? Do you know who you are? If you don't know or you need a refresher, let me remind you:

You are loved! "For God so loved the world that he gave his one and only Son, that whoever believes in him shall not perish but have eternal life." (John 3:16 NIV)

You are chosen! "For he chose us in him before the creation of the world to be holy and blameless in his sight." (Ephesians 1:4 NIV)

You are claimed! "See what great love the Father has lavished on us, that we should be called children of God! And that is what we are! The reason the world does not know us is that it did not know him." (1 John 3:1 NIV)

You are redeemed and forgiven! "In him we have redemption through his blood, the forgiveness of sins, in accordance with the riches of God's grace." (Ephesians 1:7 NIV)

You are well-known! "Before I formed you in the womb, I knew you, before you were born, I set you apart..." (Jeremiah 1:5 NIV)

You are victorious! "I have told you these things, so that in me you may have peace. In this world you will have trouble. But take heart! I have overcome the world." (John 16:33 NIV)

You have purpose! "In him we were also chosen, having been predestined according to the plan of him who works out everything in conformity with the purpose of his will, in order that we, who were the first to put our hope in Christ, might be for the praise of his glory." (Ephesians 1:11-12 NIV)

Your dash matters! You matter! Because you are here, your life has a purpose that only you can fulfill. You may wonder if you are able to accomplish your dreams and walk in your purpose but let me assure you that you can! Say goodbye to the days of wondering if you can do this or that. Stop wondering and start knowing. Maybe you don't have the support from others that you think you need. It's okay; you have God, and you have you. Philippians 4:13 says, "I can do all this through Him who gives me strength." (NIV) Realize that you're not operating out of your own ability but rather His ability. Your strength is in Him.

The other day, I looked at myself in the mirror and I began to talk to me. I spoke over my life to myself, and it was a powerful experience. It felt strange at first, but there I was looking myself dead in my eyes, speaking against the doubt, the fear, and anxiety. I reminded myself of my purpose and of the power that resided in me. There will be enough negativity coming from outside sources. We don't need to be an additional source of negativity for ourselves. Speak positively with assurance of who you are. Support and push yourself. You are more than enough.

DREAM AND DO

When it comes to going after your dreams, never let anyone stop you. Be it lack of support, lack of confidence, or whatever the case may be, keep pushing to make them a reality. I recall a time when one of my lifetime friends was going to help me with a certain project I was working on. I needed her to create a logo for me because I didn't have that skill set. Even though, my friend's plate was full, she agreed to help me. Some time passed and I hadn't heard anything from her.

During a conversation a while later, she broke down and told me that due to her hectic schedule, she just couldn't help me. She felt bad for not being able to, but I understood. In that moment, she told me that when going for my dreams, never ever let anyone (even her) stop me from fulfilling them. Your dreams will never be as big to others as they are to you. You are responsible for making them come true. We cannot place the responsibility of fulfilling our dreams with someone else who can't even see the vision.

Your vision and your dash matter! They are important to you and to those attached to you. Someone needs to hear your story, be blessed by your gift, and even pour back into you. So, get your birthing plan together. Nourish your dream with the right foods for it to grow in your belly. Plan, plan, plan. No one can do it for you because your vision, your dream is growing inside YOU. When labor day comes, no one can birth your babies for you. That is your responsibility. Gain control of yourself and of your thoughts. Stay on top of your contractions. Slow your breathing. Remember that you're amazing and you're doing an awesome job. You got this! Now PUSH!

Chapter Five
All Dashes Matter

While growing up in a Christian home, I was taught to treat others as I would want to be treated. Unfortunately, at times, I allowed fear of what people thought keep me from being more outgoing, opening up, and even having conversations with them. I never wanted to come off as what some would say "stuck up" or even mean. I just kept to myself because of fear, possible lack of self-confidence, and because I didn't want to get into trouble.

I can recall the very first open house or parent teacher conference that I attended in kindergarten. I was so excited for my parents to see all my work, my table and seat, and my accomplishments so far in kindergarten. I remember taking my parents around the classroom to show them all the delightful things that I was excited about. I specifically remember taking them to the housekeeping center. Oh, the joys of being a child again.

After their brief tour, it was time to speak with my teacher. As I sat there, I remember the teacher singing my praises to my parents. There was one particular comment that stuck out to me. She said, "She is a little chatterbox." I remember beaming in that "compliment" because I had no idea what a chatterbox was, and because I never really got into trouble at school, I didn't think it was a bad thing. But all of a sudden, my dad gave me a look and I sank in my seat. I began to worry because I then realized that a chatterbox might not be a good thing. Oh Lord!

When the conference was over, I remember my dad telling me that I needed to stop doing so much talking in school. Because of his influence on me and reverence I had for him; I knew that I did not want to be a chatterbox any longer, especially if it meant that I would get into trouble. I did not fool with the Bishop. After that, I was probably one of the quietest in my class until I graduated from high school. Even in college, I kept to myself for the most part.

This quietness has probably kept me out of quite a bit of trouble. I usually just minded my business in school and in most other places. You see, many times, we mind other people's business instead of our own, and we lose focus as a result. On the other side of this, my quietness actually kept me from being outgoing and in some way, shape, or form, I never fit in. There were a few who had their thoughts about me and voiced their opinions. They weren't the nicest things to say, but at that time, I just wanted to get through the day and go home. Never did I think I was better than anyone else, I just couldn't do what most everyone else did. I knew that there would be consequences for my actions.

This even poured over into the relationships I had with youth at the church. Sometimes I would get into trouble because I was not allowed to talk with friends during service. They would tell me I was stuck up, that I thought I was better than them just because my father was the pastor, amongst so many other things, all of which I just accepted. What they didn't understand was that if I decided to go ahead and play around or talk with them, there was a consequence after service that I did not want.

At one of our church conventions, I believe I was around 13 or 14 years old, there was a mall connected to the hotel in which we lodged. After the morning service, I wanted to go to the mall with my friends. I distinctly remember there being a church fashion show scheduled directly after service. I didn't want to go to the fashion show because my friends asked me to go to the mall with them. I asked my parents if I could go to the mall. My father told me I couldn't because I needed to be in church. I thought to myself, *It's not even a service, it's a fashion show! Why do I have to sit through a fashion show?!* I was heated. I questioned him and I recall him becoming very stern and saying, "You cannot always go and do what everyone else is doing."

So, there I stood, trying to figure out how I was going to tell those waiting for me that I couldn't go. This would be even more reason for them to talk. That was like the ba-zillionth time (yes, I'm exaggerating) that I couldn't do something because of what someone else would say or because of the flack my father might've caught if I were being a kid/teenager, or God forbid, a human being. There was much that came along with being a PK. Yes, being a Preacher's/Pastor's Kid usually wasn't fun. I'm sure my fellow PKs and I could compile a rather lengthy book about it. Many will be able to relate to this piece of my story and I to theirs.

Everyone has a story. There are a countless number of circumstances and backgrounds from which we all come. We will never understand all of them, so why is it that we are quick to judge or assume and slow to gain understanding? That person who is bitter has gone through something to be that way. The one who is usually full of smiles may not even be happy. The panhandler on the corner could be very well off while the person driving the Benz may be struggling to make ends meet. You never know what a person has gone through, is going through, or will go through. However, you always know how you want to be treated, so treat them that way.

TAKE THE TIME

One day, I was leaving therapy, and I headed to Chipotle as usual. I learned of a new location down the street from my therapist's office a few weeks prior, so I figured I would go to that one this day. When I walked in, I was the only Chipotle-a-holic there; this was a rare phenomenon. Delighted, I walked right up and ordered my food. As I was checking out, the cashier said, "It's a really gloomy day outside." My radar automatically went up without my consent. So, I replied, "But it's a day, and I'd rather have that versus the alternative." The cashier sort of chuckled and agreed with me. While sort of slowly shrugging her shoulders, she proceeded to say, "I just need something to look forward to." Upon hearing that, the alarms, bells, and whistles went off in my head and my heart sank because she felt like that. I knew how she felt. I had been there before, many times. I knew what *that* sadness felt like. I knew those feelings and I did not want her to feel that. I knew she had purpose, but she needed to know that.

Before I knew it, I just let what was naturally in me come out. I said, "What about later today or tomorrow? You have that to look forward to!" She sat there and just looked at me like that didn't seem good enough. *Oh, this poor girl,* I thought to myself. I just so happened to have a book with me that I'd been reading in my purse to share with her. I said, "I have something for you." I pulled the book out of my purse, and I told her to write the title and the author's name down. "Go get this book as soon as you can and read it. It is life changing." She wrote down the information and replied, "Really?" I said, "Yes! Read it as soon as you can." She smiled for the first time since I'd been in there.

PLANT POSITIVE SEEDS

Take the time to listen to and see other people. Even when they're not saying anything, they are. Many times, we can be in such a rush that we miss an opportunity to make a positive impact on or plant a positive seed in someone's life. We can be so selfish that we don't care what our dash reflects as long as we benefit. If you want to have a fulfilling life, you must first learn to be selfless, supportive and helpful to others. Be of service to someone else along the road of life and see how your life changes for the better.

We are always planting seeds through our communication. We constantly (verbally and nonverbally) communicate. Simply holding a door for the person coming out the store behind you communicates that you've considered them. If a man holds a door for an unfamiliar woman, it may communicate that he's interested in her or that it's simply a part of his social makeup. If he is interested, he has a higher chance of receiving positive feedback from that woman by holding the door versus not. The gentleman planted a positive seed through his nonverbal communication. If the woman is in turn interested in him, that seed will be watered through further communication between the pair.

When we were children, our parents, guardians, families, teachers, mentors, and friends all planted seeds within us through their communication. Unfortunately, some of these seeds were negative. We must learn how to uproot the negative seeds, even if they have flourished into full grown plants, and replace them with positive seeds.

HUMBLE LIVING AND AWARENESS

One of the most positive seeds that we can plant within ourselves is humility. The other day, I watched a time-lapse video of a kidney bean after it was planted. The roots of the seed began to grow down into the soil. They grew deeper and flourished downwards. After the roots grew strong enough to sustain upward growth, the seed grew up and emerged out of the soil. If I had been looking at the soil on the surface level only, I would've never seen all the growth and establishment being made underground. If the roots were shallow or hadn't grown at all, the breakthrough of the actual plant at the surface may not have occurred. If it did occur, the plant may not have lasted long because the roots were not strong enough to sustain the growth.

I am reminded of the scripture that says, "Humble yourselves, therefore, under God's mighty hand, that he may lift you up in due time." (I Peter 5:6 NIV) We must grow down(wards) in order to grow up(wards)! We shouldn't concern ourselves with being prideful and boastful, but rather with staying low and allowing God to lift us up. Learn to continually live at the feet of Jesus. There is power in humility.

One of the easiest ways to practice humility is to serve others. Take initiative in helping someone. Give an encouraging word. Do something you wouldn't normally do/out of the ordinary to build someone else up. For many, this could be to speak a kind word to a complete stranger. A few weeks ago, I was walking on the treadmill at my local gym. There was a lady on the treadmill next to me. I listened as she panted for air and grunted through her physical challenge. She kept pushing even though it sounded like she wanted to give up. I thought to myself, *Go girl!* In that moment, I wanted to encourage her. I hesitated because I didn't want to make her feel uncomfortable. Other fearful excuses quickly came to mind as to why I shouldn't encourage her. Not long after, her machine stopped. Before I knew it, "You did a great job!" came out of my mouth. She looked up, smiled, and said, "Thank you!"

What harm could come from encouraging someone? What damage was done speaking a positive word into her life? None. None at all. In fact, I don't know what sort of day she was having, if anyone had taken the time to pay attention to her, or if she needed an encouraging boost. At any given time, everyone can use more encouragement and more positivity in their lives. Raising our awareness of what we communicate, verbally and nonverbally, is crucial. As stated before, we constantly communicate through what we do and don't say, and through our actions or lack thereof. We must also be aware of what others are communicating to us. At times throughout my life, I have been ignorant of the fact that I'm just not as important to some as they are verbally communicating me to be. Most, if not all of us have heard the saying, "Actions speak louder than words." A person can tell someone how much they mean to them, but if their actions don't back up their speech, it invalidates their words.

Many years ago, a guy who I was dating asked me if I would ever consider going tanning. Mind you, I am a very fair-skinned individual, and I burn easily in sun exposure, all of which he was aware. When he asked me that question, I told him that I wasn't sure that I would ever go because of all the risks involved and because I was happy with the color of my skin. He said that there were lotions that I could apply. I wouldn't even have to be exposed to the UV lights or radiation. In my young mind I thought, *Maybe I should consider it if it's that important to him.* After the thought, I told him that I would consider it. I even bought some of the tanning lotions that make you look a couple shades darker.

Further into the relationship, he asked me what I absolutely had to have in a mate. I gave him my little list and it included details about how I needed my mate to be God-fearing, loving, and kind, just to name a few. When I finished, he proceeded to share his absolutes with me. His included things about how his mate MUST ALWAYS have fresh breath, about her grooming, and many other physical details. While he was speaking, I thought about how my breath isn't ALWAYS fresh and how my legs aren't always freshly shaven. *Hmmm. I guess he's not fully describing me because I don't meet all his physical absolutes. This list is pretty shallow*, I thought to myself.

I told these stories because many months later, I looked back, and I realized just what he was communicating to me. He wanted me to change to make him happy. He was not happy with who I was. In one breath, he would tell me that he loved me, but in the other, he was trying to change me. At the time, I wasn't even aware of it, and I thought if I wanted to keep him, I'd better conform to fit his image. I'm grateful that I gave it some thought afterwards, and I was secure enough within myself to know better.

We must be aware of what we allow and adhere to in our dashes. Don't ever let anyone attempt to change you. On the other hand, don't try to change anyone else. That's not their or our job. Each dash is unique and we all have our own story. No person is inferior or superior to the next. We all matter. All dashes matter.

Chapter Six
What's in Your Dash?

———

THROW THESE AWAY and continue to do so as they try to invade your space:

IS CONFUSION IN YOUR DASH?

A group of friends and I went out to dinner one evening. There was one particular individual who was new to the group. As introductions were being made, their name sounded familiar to me. When I sat down, I began to remember why it was familiar and how I knew who they were. As we were leaving the restaurant, this individual questioned me about how I knew them, but they didn't know me. I explained that we had a mutual acquaintance. With a look of concern, their reply was "don't believe what you've heard."

After this encounter, the thought crossed my mind that I never want to be the type of person who has to give this sort of response. Think about this, "A good name is more desirable than great riches; to be esteemed is better than silver or gold." (Proverbs 22:1 NIV) People won't remember many things that you say, but they will always remember what you do. None of us have ever done everything right and we will never do every single thing right; we are human. However, we have the power to change and constantly replace confusion with clarity.

I associate the word confusion with drama. At what point in life do we let go of the confusion and live a clear, drama free life? I don't think we realize how detrimental confusion can really be. The effects of confusion include: impaired decision making, loss of the ability to recognize people (including yourself) or places, and unclear thinking due to a change in mental status.

God is not the author of confusion; Satan is. He will have your mind so twisted that you won't even realize it's him behind it. You will think you're operating through your own will, but he's working behind the scenes, putting things in your head that are appealing, all the while trying to destroy you. You won't even recognize that you're identifying with someone who isn't even you. He will have you thinking that you came up with that idea to walk away from the person you love to be with the person you lust. Reevaluate. He will whisper in your ear that prayer does not work, but you know it was God who kept you from losing it. He will have you questioning God's validity and existence if you're not careful. Satan will try it, but **don't let your perplexion override your perception; remember who God is. Dismiss confusion.**

IS JEALOUSY IN YOUR DASH?

When we look at other people, sometimes the desire to want what we think they have creeps in. From there, we may start to compare. As long as we are focused on others, we are not focused on ourselves. To overcome jealousy, we must first realize that blessings are tailor-made.

Have you ever gotten a prescription filled? On the label of that prescription is your name, address, birthdate, and prescription details. Amongst these details, is a warning: "Caution: Federal law prohibits the transfer of this drug to any person other than the patient for whom it was prescribed." This prescription belongs to a specific person and ONLY to them. In the event that someone else takes it, the consequences could be grave. Their body may not be able to handle the medicine in that specific dosage.

The avenue through which someone is blessed is tailor-made for that specific person. Other people may not be able to handle what they went through to get where they are and to have what they have. We are not equipped to handle other people's situations. We are equipped to handle our own situations. Once they've gone through whatever it may be, there's a tailor-made blessing attached to the other side of their struggle. We normally don't think about or even see their struggle; we just see their blessing and desire it. We don't see the hell they went through to get where they are today. We just see the outcome of them making it through.

Attached to your tailor-made struggle is a tailor-made blessing that only you can access and that no one else can have. I don't know about you, but I want what's for me. I want my specific blessings. I don't want your prescription; I want mine! No, I don't want your dash; I want mine. I don't desire your success because it's not mine. I want the success I have and that I'm going after. I don't want any of your stuff; I just want mine. So, you can keep that, I'm good!

IS DOUBT IN YOUR DASH?

On May 22, 2018, my clock rang at 6:00 am and I hit snooze. I told myself I would get up and go to the gym. I had been going at this time for a couple of weeks, trying to beat everyone else from waking up. I noticed how my day was better as a result of releasing endorphins and having that one-on-one time in worship while walking on the treadmill. Snooze expired and I got up at 6:08 am. I was proud that I got up and got ready for the gym because I was up until after 1 o'clock in the morning the night before. I pushed through my tiredness because I knew that my body would physically, mentally, and psychologically benefit from exercising.

Before leaving, I had to write a letter of encouragement for my oldest daughter because it was End-of-Grade Testing week. As I was getting ready and even while putting my shoes on, I fought the urge to just lay back in bed. Hubby was snoring and looked so comfortable in that bed, but I kept pushing. While driving to the gym, I listened to *Get*

Up Mornings with Erica Campbell. On this particular morning, it seemed like I got in the car and turned on the radio at the perfect moment.

God began to speak to me through Erica. She spoke about how she trusted God completely and how we could do all things through Christ who strengthens us. She continued on to say that it doesn't matter what people say or about their fears, keep trusting God and know that you can do anything He has given you to do. If He gave it to you, you can do it. It doesn't matter if no one else has ever done it before, you will be the first. It doesn't matter if you feel that you don't have the ability, you have the ability through God; you have His strength. It brought to mind my favorite scripture, II Corinthians 12:9 "...My grace is sufficient for you, for my power is made perfect in weakness."

I was so encouraged after listening to that segment that I wanted to call into the show and let her know that she sparked something in me. I felt renewed and encouraged to keep going with that which the Lord had given me. I wasn't sure that I would get through, but I am grateful that God used her specifically for me on that day. It was nothing new or something that I was unfamiliar with, but given everything that I had been struggling with, especially the day before, God sent that word for me. I told God that if I ever got to speak to or meet Erica Campbell that I would tell her how she blessed me, and I would encourage her. I will come back to this later.

God began to minister to me throughout the whole morning and I received what I needed to keep going. One of the things He dropped in my mind was, "The fact that I can't see it, means ABSOLUTELY NOTHING. #it'snotwhatisee." I made a Facebook post about it because that word spoke so deeply to me. I was thinking, *Okay, I know I can do it through You Jesus, but I can't see it; I just don't see how Lord. I don't have the resources, I don't know how to word everything, who would edit the book, how will it get published, will it reach the masses, will it change and help someone who struggled like me, will it give someone fuel to keep going?* I wanted emotions to be evoked and brought out, the devil exposed, and for people to be victorious. I wanted them to use this book as a weapon and reference to make it through. This was in reference to this book and to another book that is in the works. I was dealing with so much it seemed: raising children effectively, being the wife and mother He wanted me to be, being more active at my church with all my children, staying positive in it all (even through disappointment, etc.), weight problems, blood pressure issues, financial problems, trying to face and deal with traumas which stemmed from losses, among too many other things to name. I thought to myself, *How am I going to write a book when I have so much else going on? How am I going to write a book period? Am I even qualified?*

Before God gave me that, He reminded me that I am being fought so hard because I am doing what He wants me to do. Satan was mad and was trying to get me to feel defeated so I would just stop. This particular Facebook post read, "So, you do realize that you're being fought so hard to discourage you from doing and accomplishing what God has for you to do, right? If you fight back and know that you can do ALL things through Christ who strengthens you, it destroys Satan's plan..He is not trying to have it? Fight back y'all! You got this!!! (Encouraging myself too!)"

I doubted, but I had to remember who and whose I was in order to combat it.

IS BUSYNESS IN YOUR DASH?

At the time of this specific doubt, I wasn't focused. I was allocating too much focus to too many areas. Remember back in YOLO Dash (Chapter 1) when I gave the title of one of my father's messages? It was: "The Main Thing is to Keep the Main Thing the Main Thing." I had too many, what I called, "main things" going on. I had to STOP. I was not happy because my focus was so off. I was super overwhelmed. Yes, I loved God. Yes, I was living for Him, but was I really focused on Him? You see when you are focused on something, you can see it clearly without any distractions. There are things that can be going on around you that you don't even pay attention to. You can see busyness with your peripheral vision, but it's not your focus.

Life happens. You have jobs, tasks, callings, meetings, conferences, spouses, significant others, children, pets, obligations, deadlines, uplines, sidelines and whatever else. When distracted by all these things God has given you, you have adjusted your lens to focus on them. I've said before that you can't see His face if your vision is compromised. If you find yourself with compromised vision, it's time to strip away some "stuff" and refocus! Throw whatever is hindering you from seeing Him clearly to the side and get back in the face of God! It's so important to keep your connection with him intact. The further away you get from Him, the harder it is to hear Him speak.

We can sing in the choir, usher, head all the auxiliaries, preach, pastor, lead others to God et cetera, but doing the work of God is not equivalent to having a relationship with God. We all have to be careful that we don't get caught up in the motions and movement of things that we neglect our relationship with Him. We have to be so careful not to overload our dashes with all the blessings of God to the point where we don't even know Him.

KEEP OR ADD THESE:

IS LOVE IN YOUR DASH?

Love is beautiful. There can be many issues that test the limits of love whether it is in a relationship you have with others or even in self-love. Declaring your love for someone and them declaring their love for you, is not enough to sustain the relationship. When hurtful arguments/fights and other negativity arises in a relationship, they have the potential to wound you. Sometimes family members or friends will not speak for years because of these wounds. Love itself, is not a band aid. You cannot simply slap it on a wound/issue and declare it healed because of love. There is work that needs to be done in order for that wound to properly heal. It needs cleaning, ointment, air, time, more cleaning, more ointment, more air, and more time. That is love, doing the work that it takes to heal the wound. Simply slapping a band aid on it to cover it and then walking away does nothing. Under the band aid, that wound is still festering and oozing. It's not healing.

Love is work, not to be thrown around lightly. Jesus put in work, so much work (mentally, physically, and psychologically) to get on the cross and die. THAT is LOVE. Love is the greatest force in the world. If you don't have love and show love in your dash, you have nothing. "...and if I have a faith that can move mountains, but do not have love, I am nothing." (I Corinthians 13:2 NIV)

Love God! "Love the Lord your God with all your heart and with all your soul and with all your mind and with all your strength." (Mark 12:30 NIV) My father used to tell me that if my vertical relationship was intact then my horizontal ones would be too. This is the absolute truth. If you love God, you will want to make Him smile. Your love for Him will help you show His love to others and to yourself! How can you show love to others and treat people right when you don't even love yourself or treat yourself right?

IS FORGIVENESS IN YOUR DASH?

Forgiveness is something that we have all been given freely. Just as we have been forgiven, we need to forgive. I have read and listened to loved ones talk about forgiveness and how it is for the weak. My heart broke as I witnessed this so far-from-the-truth statement being uttered. Contrarily, forgiveness is for the strong and courageous! Forgiveness is not for the person forgiven but rather for the one forgiving. It sets us free from the prison we created. We may not ever get that duly owed apology we want. Many times, we will have to forgive without the offender even realizing that they've offended. On the other hand, when we do receive an apology, be quick to forgive. "Blessed are the merciful, for they will be shown mercy." (Matthew 5:7 NIV) "For if you forgive other people when they sin against you, your heavenly Father will also forgive you." (Matthew 6:14 NIV)

When my mom was sick, a family friend came over to visit her. As we were sitting around the living room talking, the friend apologized for not coming sooner to see about her. The thing that sticks out in my mind about that conversation was my mom's response. She simply looked up, raised her hand, and said, "I find no fault." She said more, but the point was that it was okay, she wasn't holding anything against him or anyone else. You never know what a person's circumstances are, what they are up against, or what they've been or are going through. So before "getting in your feelings" about other people, have compassion and forgive how you want to be forgiven. This doesn't mean that you're a doormat or have to maintain toxic relationships. You can forgive and proceed to love from a distance. You can't change a person, nor are you responsible for their actions. You can only change yourself and are responsible and accountable for YOU.

Stop lying awake at night trying to figure out how to get revenge. Don't dwell on the offense or the offender. The individual who "wronged" you may be living their best dash while not even thinking about you or your grudge. Why give someone that much control over your thoughts and that much power over your life? How is it that we can hold things against people, but God forgives them? Are we greater than God? Certainly not!

Please understand that we must grant ourselves this same forgiveness. Some of us have a tendency to beat ourselves up over mistakes, great or small. I remember sitting in church one day and I allowed something I'd done to keep me down. My sadness was evident while sitting in that service. After church, someone came up to me and encouraged me to pick my head up. The conversation was short, but very powerful. Over time, I grasped the importance of self forgiveness. How is it that we can hold things against ourselves, but God forgives us? Are we greater than God? Certainly not!

IS EXPECTANCY IN YOUR DASH?

I'd like to add two questions to that one: How's your posture? Are you looking for God in everything? Get into position to receive all God has for you! Each day, live your dash in anticipation and fervently look for Him in your life. You may chalk things up to coincidence without realizing that it is God moving in your life. When you really seek His face daily, you will find Him.

How is it that two people can hear the same message/word, and it affects one of them and not the other? One of them is inspired and refreshed afterwards and the other, not so much. My conclusion is that they are postured differently. The first one was looking for something with an open heart while the other one may have been going through the motions but not really expecting to hear something for them.

While looking through my father's Bible I came across a note he wrote, "What we receive from God is directly related to what we expect from Him (based on His Word)." You see, I don't want to simply exist; I must thrive! The only way I know how to thrive is to have hope and posture myself to receive what I expect.

I expect God to be everything to me that he promised. He is our refuge. He is our strength. He is an ever-present help in times of trouble. He is our glory and the lifter of our heads. He is our provider. He is our peace. He is our way maker. He is our Father. Our Father wants ongoing communion with us.

I also expect Him to do what He promised. He promised that He would never leave nor forsake us. He delivers us from all of our afflictions. He promised that if we delight ourselves in Him, He will give us the desires of our hearts. He promised us rest, peace, strength, joy, beauty for ashes. We can take our messed-up situations and release them to Him, knowing that He has a plan and that we can trust Him. Stay in posture to receive and have full confidence in Him. Wake up every morning looking to see how He is going to move in your life.

ARE GRATEFULNESS AND APPRECIATION IN YOUR DASH?

One huge way that I have learned to be happy is to be grateful. If you adopt an attitude of gratitude and be thankful for even the smallest of things, happiness will find you. We cannot find our happiness in others; it's personal. You are responsible for your own happiness. Find it in the little things. If you don't, you'll be an unhappy person while waiting for those big things.

"Be thankful for what you have; you'll end up having more. If you concentrate on what you don't have, you will never, ever have enough." (-Oprah Winfrey) This quote, stated by the beautiful Oprah Winfrey, speaks volumes. When you are **thankful** and focus on what you have, you can do so much more. Do what you can with what you have! The day will come when you can do more if you use what you have now.

Appreciate what you have. Show **appreciation** when others do for you. Don't take kind gestures for granted, whether giving or receiving. Through you may be the only way someone sees God or experiences the love of God.

IS POSITIVITY IN YOUR DASH?

Have you ever had someone say something crazy to you? I mean, they just let something come out that makes you wonder why they even opened their mouth. Yes? I have too. When I was growing up, I remember going to the shoe store with my mother. I needed a pair of dress shoes. I picked a pair that I really liked; I thought they were stylish. I couldn't have been more than 12 or 13 years old. I wore my new shoes to church one day and after service, someone significantly older than me, came up to me and said, "Those shoes are *really* ugly." This is one of those times, even at my tender age, I realized that some people don't have a) common sense or b) a filter. This person's unwarranted comment was not a joke. They were serious. You may wonder why I shared this story. Well, there are several ways I could go with this. Predominantly, I shared it because there are people that we will just have to dismiss.

We have to learn to **dismiss negativity**. Anything that comes to interrupt your positivity should be dismissed. Let's talk about other dismissals while we're here. There are posts and comments on Facebook and Instagram that we will have to just dismiss. Every person, every post, every comment, or every question (on or off social media) does not subpoena a response. You can see something you don't agree with and not give your opinion. You may have an opinion, but it doesn't always need to be voiced.

There is so much negativity that we will involuntarily and sometimes voluntarily encounter on a daily basis. Checking the thoughts that are in our own heads is important. Once we are aware of the negative thinking, we are prone to have, we can then change it with positive thinking. There is a book I will mention below to help with this. **Combat negativity with positivity**.

IS INTENTIONALITY IN YOUR DASH?

Be intentional in your dash. Think things through. Really ask yourself, "Why?" "Why do I want this?" "Why do I want to say or do this?" "What good will come from it?" "Do I actually need this?" Really think about if and how "this" and "it" matter. Be intentionally thankful, appreciative, and positive.

Have you ever driven home, pulled in your driveway and realized you don't remember the drive home? It can be a little alarming when you really think about it. Like, "Did I run any red lights?" "Was I speeding?" You can be so used to doing something that it's ingrained in your memory. It becomes such a habit that it doesn't mean to you what it once did. You say, "I love you" or "I love you too," but is there weight behind your words or are you just on autopilot like that drive home? Be certain you're not just going through the motions. Mean what you say and say what you mean. Don't become comfortable in habits where you miss out on life. Take the time to think about your life and areas in which you may just be on autopilot. Flip the switch and be intentional in your dash.

IS WISDOM IN YOUR DASH?

During therapy, my therapist told me about a book that he wanted me to read. Two days later, I went to Barnes and Noble, purchased the book, and I began reading that evening. I want to recommend this book to you. As a matter of fact, I don't just want to recommend it, I am asking you to please purchase it and read it. Your dash can be forever changed.

In *What to Say When You Talk to Your Self* by Shad Helmstetter, PhD, you will learn new techniques to improve the quality of your life, and these techniques are simple and free! After I read the first chapter or two of this book, I immediately began to make changes in my life, ultimately affecting those around me for the better. I saw and heard things differently, even those thoughts in my mind changed. During one of my reading sessions, I read "If I cannot affect it or direct it-I accept it." (-Shad Helmstetter) It reminded me of the Serenity Prayer that I spoke of in Chapter 1. The things we cannot change are out of our control (the past, for example), so we cannot affect or direct it. The things we can change (affect or direct) include our thoughts and our futures. When we keep everything in perspective, we will have the wisdom to know the difference. In the last chapter, I spoke about how we need to uproot any negative seeds in our lives and replace them with positive seeds. This book will give you complete instructions about how to do that. If you'd like to add more wisdom to your dash, please go grab it, read it and apply it to your life. You WILL NOT be sorry!

IS CONFIDENCE IN YOUR DASH?

So, let's move back to my Erica Campbell story. Before, I said that I told God that if I ever got to speak to or meet Erica Campbell, I would tell her how she blessed me, and I would encourage her. The same evening I said this, I received a message on Facebook Messenger from who appeared to be Erica Campbell. My heart began to pound. I could not believe that she messaged little ole' me. The message was a pretty general greeting. In disbelief, I asked if it was really her! "She" replied, "Yes, it is really me dear." Looking back, I was so naïve. I just couldn't get over that. I had just told the Lord this same morning that I wanted to encourage her and now the opportunity had presented itself. I had never inboxed her or reached out any other way before. I didn't even know how to get in contact with her. So, my mind was blown that she reached out to me, so I thought.

I began telling "her" what happened that day, how she encouraged me, and so on. I never received a reply. So, I started doing some browsing. Whoever this person was, was very creative. They used the same profile picture that was on Erica's real profile and the page looked so similar to the real one. Then I remembered to look for the blue check mark. Was it there? NO! My heart wanted to be disappointed, but I said that if it's meant for me to tell her, it'll be. I have to admit that it didn't sit well with me, but the more I thought about it, the more I thought how crazy it was and that it might not have been such the coincidence I thought.

The next morning, I got up early again to go to the gym. I sat in the gym parking lot, and I heard information about calling in to speak with Erica about her Faith Walk. I immediately called in and got right through. After I gave my name and my location, I heard, "Please hold for Erica." Oh. My. Goodness! I sat there amazed. I tried to gather my thoughts about how I would tell her. I didn't want to stumble over my words. I wanted to make sure I didn't become long-winded like some other callers I'd listened to before. My mind started racing. A few moments later, she picked up my line and I spoke with her. We spoke briefly and I was able to let her know how much she encouraged me. This may not seem like anything much to some, but to me, it meant a whole lot. I put my confidence in God, and I knew that if it was His Will, it would happen.

Not only should we be confident in God, we should also have self-confidence. I know I've repeated how crucial it is to remember who and whose you are. If you don't know who you are, you will be easily swayed and influenced. I read somewhere that if you don't know who you are, someone else will tell you.

DO YOU HAVE CONTROL IN YOUR DASH?

When you give your control over to outside sources, you are aborting your potential. You are no longer operating you, that outside source is. How can you reach your greatest potential and live your dash to the fullest, if you're not in control of you? It's simple, you cannot.

Is it fear that has control in your dash? Tell fear to get outta here! God didn't give it to you, so it has to go! What about confusion? Jealousy? Doubt? Oh, I know...busyness? If any of these have been in control of you, it's time to serve them their walking papers.

Do you know who's in control of you? Do you know who's in control of your thoughts? If the answer to both of these questions isn't "I am," promote yourself and take over! You are in control. If you feel like you've lost your control, rest assured that you can get it back. Right now!

Back in Chapter 1, I spoke of how if I had any regrets, it would be that at various points in my life, I had given control of my thoughts over to outside sources. When my mom died, I gave control of my dash over to anger, sadness, confusion, loneliness and the list goes on. I allowed these things to consume me to the point where they even controlled my actions and not just my thoughts. Until I took my control back, I was a sad sight on the inside. My outside looked just fine, and I could smile in your face while on the inside, I was torn to pieces. This is no way to live. I was simply existing but not thriving. When I took it back, I started to heal and after much work, eventually thrive.

You were not created to simply exist. Don't you know that you have purpose? Don't you know that you are extraordinary? You do and you are. There is beauty in your uniqueness. There has never been and will never be another you. You have been fearfully and wonderfully made. Don't be easily broken or manipulated by the words, actions, or negative influences of others, but be assured in yourself and who YOU are called to be. It is time to stop looking at those around you and focus on you. Take control as only you can, THRIVE, and LIVE **YOUR BEST DASH**!

Chapter Seven
Living My BEST DASH Declarations

- The past is history, but my future is not a mystery!

- I no longer dwell in the past but rather thrive in my now and towards my future!

- I am living my dash to the fullest!

- My dash may not look like other dashes, and it shouldn't. I am unique, extraordinary, and one of a kind!

- My dash is golden! I will treat it as such!

- I will go to counseling. There is nothing wrong with it. The stigmas connected to it are bogus!

- I will live in such a way that I am a happier, healthier, and whole me!

- My dash is my own priority!

- I don't wait for anyone to make me happy; no one else has that type of control over me!

- I don't live in confusion, fear, or anxiety! I do live in love, power, and clarity. I have peace of mind and self-control!

- I do not seek to be validated by people. God validates me and I only seek to please Him!

- Living humbly does not make me weak! There is power in my humility!

- I am well-known!

- I am purposed!

- I am worthy!

- I am loved!

- I am redeemed and forgiven!

- I am chosen!

- I am victorious!

- I will live my best dash!

Are You Living YOUR Best Dash?
by Mariesa L. Moore-Gentry

You only get one of these special things.
When starting out, you have no idea what it will bring.
Unaware that you're even in
Something in which you have to depend
On people for your every need
Until you're old enough to take heed
Of everything that you've been taught or lack thereof
You have to be better and rise above.
People.

People come and people go.
For quite some time that's been my motto.
As cold as this motto may seem it puts it all in perspective.
There will be those who are there for a season.
Sometimes we feel like they were there for no reason.
You learn something from everyone.
Whether they're lifetime, one time, or pop in and out,
Don't allow them to consume you with their fear and doubt.
There will be those who show you nothing but love.
They're genuine, kind, and really care,
But then you have those that say they care but stare.
Stare in jealousy while they look at your life
All the while wishing you nothing but strife.
Negativity and discord have no place in my dash.
It may be hard, harsh or rash....but
I don't care who or where it comes from it has to go.
So long, buh-bye, you don't live here no mo'!
People.

Yes, they can be something,
But what about that other being?
You. Yourself. Your body and your mind.
How do you keep yourself in line?
Sometimes we can be our biggest critic,
Not allowing ourselves to heal, celebrate or enjoy our own
skin that we're in.
Always consumed with what we don't have
All the while not being fully grateful for what we do.
Don't take your life, health, and strength for granted.
You could've awakened this day and not had it.
What if you didn't awaken at all?
Do you have any regrets, big or small?

Did you not appreciate those people in your life,
Who encouraged you, were there for you,
Letting you know everything would be alright?
Did you focus on some good but mostly just the bad and the
ugly?

Maybe you were fixated on those who treated you roughly?
That's not a good mindset to have
When you're trying to make it through your dash.
Paint yourself a different color, not just green or blue.
Make sure you love on yourself and to you be true.
My son once told me that red is a leader.
It's the first color of a rainbow, so it leads.
Control your mind and tell it which way to go.
If it starts to lead you down a wrong path, tell it NO!
Yes, it may be easier said than done
But it has to be done so the victory can be won.

Be red, take action, take control.
You are not anyone else's puppet;
You're not Kermit or any other muppet.
So, don't sit by and just sip on your tea.
Be helpful, encourage, and guide others to see.
There's more to this life than pain and guilt
It's okay to seek help, there's nothing wrong with it.
God gave us faith but also common sense.
Take it one day at a time.
Make it time well spent.
Don't ever let anyone make you feel bad
For doing what you have to do.
After all this is YOUR dash.
Live it to the fullest!

It may not look like his or hers,
but don't compare your story to theirs.
Each dash and each person is different.
There will be those who don't understand you and who you
don't understand.
That's okay. Be okay with that.
It's not a bad thing; don't let it be a setback.
You're not going to please everyone
Or always be in high demand.
Just show His love in all that you do,
And He will surely show up for you.
With anything you do
Just remember that each day is anew,

A new opportunity to get it right;
A new day to conquer any fright.
He didn't give us the spirit of fear,
So, when it comes, tell it to get outta here!
I have power, love and a sound mind!
"So, Satan, go ahead and get thee behind!"
No one will stop me from fulfilling my purpose,
Although sometimes you may wonder if it's even worth it.
Let me assure you it really, really is.
Keep pushing, keep pursuing, stay in your own biz.
Stay focused and know that you can always depend
On He who created you, you will always have a friend.

Dashes contain
Ups, Downs
Wins, Defeats
Gains, Losses
Life, Death
Happiness, Sadness
And so much more
We really don't know what's in store.
One thing that we can be sure of
And this I say proud,
Dash is life
And life is loud!
It may be loud with excitement, happiness or glee.
Or sometimes the silence screams...wanting to be free.
Whatever your dash is screaming, embrace it or erase it.
Erase the bad, and replace it with good
Even if you are misunderstood.
You are only responsible for you,
So, let them look, and do what you do.
Dash is life
And life is loud!
Live Your Best Dash and make yourself proud!

LET'S STAY CONNECTED!

———

Thank you so much for purchasing my book! I pray that it has inspired, encouraged and uplifted you. I welcome your feedback and review of the book. I would love for us to stay connected. Follow me on social media:

Facebook and Instagram: @yourbestdash

If you are interested in my Life Coaching services, please visit my website and/or send me an email.

Website: www.yourbestdash.com

Email: yourbestdash@gmail.com

Remember, you were not created to live a mediocre life, but you were created for a purpose that only you can fulfill. It's time to thrive! I look forward to hearing from you soon.

Mariesa